高等职业教育
旅游类专业
系列教材

中国特色高水平专业群建设成果

U0719669

乘务员头等舱餐饮及播音艺术

主　编　王建惠　刘清华
副主编　武贤伟　刘嘉晨　朱玉玺

西安交通大学出版社
XI'AN JIAOTONG UNIVERSITY PRESS

图书在版编目（CIP）数据

乘务员头等舱餐饮及播音艺术：汉文、英文／王建惠，刘清华主编. — 西安：西安交通大学出版社，2022.11

ISBN 978 - 7 - 5693 - 2718 - 2

Ⅰ. ①乘…　Ⅱ. ①王…②刘…　Ⅲ. ①民用航空—乘务人员—饮食业—商业服务—汉、英 ②民用航空—乘务人员—播音—语言艺术—汉、英　Ⅳ. ①F560.9

中国版本图书馆 CIP 数据核字（2022）第 130430 号

Chengwuyuan Toudengcang Canyin ji Boyin Yishu

书　　名	乘务员头等舱餐饮及播音艺术
主　　编	王建惠　刘清华
策划编辑	张明玥
责任编辑	张明玥　卢婧雅
责任校对	张　欣
出版发行	西安交通大学出版社
	（西安市兴庆南路 1 号　邮政编码 710048）
网　　址	http://www.xjtupress.com
电　　话	（029）82668357　82667874（市场营销中心）
	（029）82668315（总编办）
传　　真	（029）82668280
印　　刷	西安五星印刷有限公司
开　　本	787 mm×1092 mm　1/16　印张 10.5　字数 252 千字
版次印次	2022 年 11 月第 1 版　2022 年 11 月第 1 次印刷
书　　号	ISBN 978 - 7 - 5693 - 2718 - 2
定　　价	43.80 元

如发现印装质量问题，请与本社市场营销中心联系。

订购热线：（029）82665248　（029）82667874

投稿热线：（029）82668804

读者信箱：phoe@qq.com

前 言

Foreword

随着中国民航业的蓬勃发展，民航业的国际化程度日益提高。航空公司对空乘人员的职业技能、职业素养和英语水平提出了较高的需求，乘务员头等舱餐饮服务和乘务员头等舱餐饮及播音艺术是乘务员对客服务工作流程中的重要环节。编写者们在总结了多年教学经验的基础上，与有多年工作经历的一线教师共同编写了本书。

本书遵循"实用为主、够用为度"的原则，力求使教材具有"实用性和可操作性"。具体而言，本书有以下两个特点：

1. 依据乘务员工作流程，为学生提供真实学习情境。

本书总体分为两部分：第一部分为乘务员头等舱餐饮服务；第二部分为机上安全和服务类广播，包括登机广播、限制使用电子装置、安全演示、客舱安全检查、颠簸广播、应急处置广播。基于机上餐饮服务和客舱广播服务情境，以具体、典型的工作任务为教学载体，进行项目化教学分析，以真实情境引导学生以任务为导向进行有效学习。

2. 实施项目任务驱动，帮助学生高效学习。

本书按照岗位工作标准和空乘人员职业资格标准制定课程学习要求，构建职业知识和能力体系。每个项目以工作任务为驱动，围绕工作任务来编排内容，注重培养学生综合应用能力以及创新解决问题的能力。

本书由陕西职业技术学院旅游与文化学院王建惠、刘清华担任主编，西北航空训练股份有限公司武贤伟、刘嘉晨、朱玉玺担任副主编。本书在编写过程中参考了近年来民航乘务方面的相关书籍及文献资料，在此对相关人员表示诚挚的谢意。由于编者水平有限，书中难免有疏漏或不妥之处，恳请专家及读者不吝指正。

编　者

2022 年 8 月

目 录

Contents

第一部分　头等舱餐饮服务

项目一　头等舱服务流程 ··· 3

　任务一　乘务员机上服务流程 SOP ································· 4

　任务二　头等舱内外场服务流程 SOP ····························· 5

项目二　头等舱餐饮服务程序 ·· 7

　任务一　远程航线餐饮服务程序 ··································· 8

　任务二　非远程航线餐饮服务程序 ································· 8

项目三　头等舱餐饮服务标准（地面） ··································· 9

　任务一　清点餐食 ··· 10

　任务二　清点机供品 ··· 10

　任务三　清点餐具车及杯车 ······································· 10

　任务四　餐饮服务预先准备 ······································· 10

　任务五　预热毛巾 ··· 11

　任务六　提供热毛巾（碟） ······································· 11

　任务七　准备迎宾饮料 ··· 11

　任务八　发放餐谱、酒水单 ······································· 12

　任务九　订餐 ··· 12

项目四　头等舱餐饮服务标准（空中） ··································· 13

　任务一　饮料及餐具准备——正餐/简餐 ·························· 14

　任务二　饮料及餐具准备——早餐 ································· 14

　任务三　饮料及餐具准备——快餐 ································· 14

任务四　餐食准备——正餐/简餐 ……………………………………… 14

任务五　餐食准备——早餐 ……………………………………………… 15

任务六　餐食准备——快餐 ……………………………………………… 15

任务七　餐食烤制注意事项 ……………………………………………… 15

任务八　面包烤制注意事项 ……………………………………………… 16

任务九　铺桌布、提供餐前饮(和果仁) ……………………………… 16

任务十　侍酒服务 ………………………………………………………… 17

任务十一　提供 CANAPE ………………………………………………… 18

任务十二　送冷盘、汤 …………………………………………………… 18

任务十三　送面包 ………………………………………………………… 18

任务十四　送主菜 ………………………………………………………… 18

任务十五　送芝士和水果 ………………………………………………… 19

任务十六　送甜品、热饮 ………………………………………………… 19

任务十七　送巧克力、餐后酒 …………………………………………… 20

任务十八　送快餐 ………………………………………………………… 20

任务十九　送早餐 ………………………………………………………… 20

任务二十　收回餐具 ……………………………………………………… 21

第二部分　乘务员播音艺术

Task 1　Check-in and Departure ………………………………………… 25

Task 2　Notice of Flight Cancellation …………………………………… 31

Task 3　Baggage Arrangement …………………………………………… 35

Task 4　Boarding …………………………………………………………… 39

Task 5　Welcome Speech ………………………………………………… 42

Task 6　Flight Route Introduction ……………………………………… 46

Task 7　Emergency Exit ………………………………………………… 50

Task 8　Safety Demonstration …………………………………………… 54

Task 9　Security Inspection ……………………………………………… 58

Task 10　Restrictions on Electronic Devices …………………………… 62

Task 11　Declaration Card ……………………………………………… 66

Task 12　Transfer Flight Information ················· 70

Task 13　Level Flight ······································ 74

Task 14　Ground Temperature ··························· 78

Task 15　Shopping ··· 82

Task 16　Meals ··· 86

Task 17　Beverages ·· 90

Task 18　Recreation ······································· 94

Task 19　Landing on the Ground ······················· 98

Task 20　Stopover ··· 102

Task 21　Landing at the Destination Airport ········· 107

Task 22　Seeing off ······································· 111

Task 23　Air Condition Problem ······················· 115

Task 24　Flight Delay Announcement ·················· 119

Task 25　Air Traffic Control ··························· 124

Task 26　Fasten the Seat Belt ·························· 129

Words and Expressions ······································ 133

Reference Answers ·· 153

第一部分

头等舱餐饮服务

项目一

头等舱服务流程

任务一　乘务员机上服务流程 SOP

时间节点	服务内容	服务行为要点标准
旅客登机前	网上准备	机组航前准备会演练
	个人准备	
	乘务准备会	
	机组协同会	
	机上准备	放置个人物品
		应急设备检查
		服务设备检查
		地面准备工作
		清舱检查
		卫生检查
		迎客前最后准备
迎客登机	准备迎客	个人形象整理
		迎客位置在位
	迎接旅客	数客
		迎客
		引导入座
		协助摆放行李
		提供服务用品
		出口座位旅客评估
舱门关闭	舱门操作	起飞前安全检查
	安全检查	
空中服务	报刊服务	按照机上服务工作任务及职业技能等级标准逐一进行分组实操及演练
	餐食烘烤	
	饮料服务	
	酒饮服务	
	餐食服务	
	回收、整理	
	细微服务和客舱管理	
落地前准备	整理客舱	下降前客舱安全检查
	安全检查	
舱门打开	舱门操作	舱门操作
落地	送客	落地后送客
	特殊旅客服务	

任务二　头等舱内外场服务流程 SOP

	内场	外场
旅客登机前	检查各自负责区域的应急设备、服务设备	
	清点机供品	检查娱乐系统
	清点餐具车、杯车	清点地服用品 布置卫生间
	清点、检查机组餐、旅客餐食 填写订餐单上餐食数量、种类	熟悉餐谱、酒水单内容 填写订餐单上旅客信息
	预热毛巾	冰镇香槟、啤酒、白葡萄酒
	服务驾驶舱	检查机组休息室
	准备用具	布置旅客个人空间
	准备迎宾饮料	摆放杂志 播放登机音乐
	清舱并汇报	
迎客服务	迎宾	
	送/收热毛巾（碟）	
	送/收迎宾饮料	
	收纳毛巾碟	发放杂志
	收纳服务用具 存放固定小推车	发放餐谱、酒水单 订餐
空中餐饮	**餐饮准备工作** ↓ **餐前饮** ↓ **小盘** ↓ **冷盘** ↓	开启烧水箱 烤制餐食、面包	开启洗手间 使用舱位/厨房分隔牌 继续未完成的订餐工作

空中餐饮	餐饮准备工作/餐前饮/小盘/冷盘		
		加热餐具	关怀旅客 服务驾驶舱
		准备酒水、冲泡热饮 准备餐前饮小推车	送热毛巾（碟） 添加保温箱内湿毛巾
		准备小食	铺桌布、提供餐前饮（和果仁）
		准备餐食车 准备中西式汤 增补餐车上的酒水饮料	提供点心 收回小食碟、整理旅客餐桌

		内场	外场
汤 ↓ 面包 ↓ 主菜 ↓ 芝士 ↓ 水果 ↓ 甜品 ↓ 热饮 ↓ 巧克力		准备面包	提供冷盘、汤
		取出冰激凌化霜	送面包，适时介绍面包种类
		整理餐车 取出加热好的餐具	收回冷荤碟和汤碗 添加饮料
		准备主菜，摆盘	提供主菜，及时添加饮料、面包
		收纳用完的餐具	合盘收回用完的餐具
		准备芝士、水果小推车	添加饮料
		增补外场所需水果和餐具	提供芝士、水果，及时提供侍酒服务
		准备甜品和热饮小推车	收回芝士、水果盘、刀叉
		收纳芝士小推车上所有物品	提供甜品和热饮
		准备巧克力、餐后酒小推车	提供巧克力、餐后酒，收回甜品盘
		准备矿泉水刀小推车	补充旅客矿泉水
		收纳服务用具	整理旅客个人空间
值班前准备		整理服装，摆放休闲小食 整理用具车，做好值班交接 调节服务舱灯光，打开服务舱工作灯	巡视客舱，关注 VIP 旅客及特殊旅客 整理客舱，布置吧台，清洁洗手间 提供铺床服务
下降前准备		清理所有储藏空间，收纳各类用具 收取驾驶舱服务用具，提供热毛巾 回收机供品、地服用品	归还旅客衣物，告知落地时间、温度 收回耳机、关闭电源、去除耳罩 整理旅客个人空间
旅客下机后各项工作		清舱检查 物品归位 地面交接	

项目二

头等舱餐饮服务程序

任务一　远程航线餐饮服务程序

正餐	简餐	早餐	快餐
订餐（若地面未完成）	订餐	订餐	订餐
送热毛巾/碟	送热毛巾/碟	送热毛巾/碟	送热毛巾、碟
铺桌布、提供餐前饮料（和果仁）	铺桌布、提前饮料	铺桌布、提供餐前饮料	铺桌布、提供餐前饮料
提供点心	提供冷盘	提供早餐餐盘	提供餐盘
提供冷盘、汤	送面包	送早餐面包	收回餐具
送面包	送主菜	送水果	
送主菜	收取餐盘	收回餐具	
收取餐盘	送水果		
送芝士和水果	收回餐具		
送甜品和热饮			
送巧克力、餐后酒			
增补矿泉水、收回餐具			
注意事项：始终关注旅客添加饮料及面包的需求，确保每次送出的是温热面包			

任务二　非远程航线餐饮服务程序

正餐/简餐/早餐
订餐（若地面未完成）
送热毛巾、碟
铺桌布、提供餐前饮料（和果仁）
合盘提供餐盘
送面包
添加饮料
收回餐具
注意事项：始终关注旅客添加饮料及面包的需求，确保每次送出的是温热面包

项目三

头等舱餐饮服务标准（地面）

任务一　清点餐食

✤机组餐

手持餐食清单，清点机组餐数量；确认有机长餐和餐具；确认其他机组成员餐食和餐具，检查餐食的质量：包装完好、餐食无异味、品质新鲜；确认餐车放入冷藏车位并打开冷藏开关。

✤旅客餐

手持餐食清单，逐一口述检查所有餐食冷盘、热食数量和餐食质量、面包的种类，并汇报；将冷盘、热食品种和数量填写在订餐单上；确认餐别，检查餐食的质量：包装完好、餐食无异味、品质新鲜；确认餐车放入冷藏车位并打开冷藏开关。

任务二　清点机供品

责任乘务员按照机供品清单，逐一检查机供品数量、质量、外包装完好、在保质期内、外部没有明显缺损。

关注当天航线来回程的餐谱与酒水清单是否齐全。

注意餐布、瓷壶、保温汤壶的数量与存放位置。

任务三　清点餐具车及杯车

根据航线性质确定用具的种类和数量(毛巾碟、中西式汤碗、饭碗、沙拉碟、瓷壶、备份餐具等)。

确认杯子数量与杯车上所附的清单一致、外观完好没有任何破损，且杯车可正常使用。

任务四　餐饮服务预先准备

✤备好服务用具
·准备好长饮杯、香槟杯、葡萄酒杯放入车内。
·准备好果仁、餐巾纸巾，使用面包篮垫布。

·准备好热饮壶、茶包、奶球、糖包、勺、搅拌棒、冰桶/夹，冷藏柠檬片。

❖备好饮料

·整合机上各类饮料（苏打水、牛奶、果汁类）将其摆放整齐，置于饮料车最上层，方便平飞后使用饮料车以提高工作效率。

❖预先备好订餐单

·提前了解旅客信息，填写到订餐单上（姓氏、喜好、特殊餐食的需要、高端旅客、VIP旅客标注）。

·将旅客冷盘、热食的数量、品种填写至订餐单。

·地面停留期间可进行订餐服务，也可在平飞后完成。

任务五　预热毛巾

毛巾碟放入保温箱底层，毛巾放入上层。

预热毛巾的温度以 40～50 ℃为宜，湿度以拧至不滴水为宜。

任务六　提供热毛巾（碟）

确认毛巾温度（温热不烫手），湿度以拧至不滴水为宜，表面平整无指印，无异味。

毛巾放入毛巾碟中，摆放美观整齐；光边在外，毛边在内；用大托盘发放时，每次不超过 10 个毛巾碟。

毛巾碟置于旅客扶手上，标识正对旅客，发送时注意手指不要碰到毛巾。

回收毛巾碟时，将毛巾碟有序摆放在托盘上并保管好，方便后续使用。

任务七　准备迎宾饮料

·冰镇香槟、啤酒、葡萄酒等。

·将一辆餐车放于 2R 门处（注意不挡住开门把手）垫上垫车布。

·上层放抽屉以及准备好的迎宾饮料，备好冰桶/夹。

·下层放置干净的长饮杯、香槟杯、葡萄酒杯以便及时添加饮料（垫好托盘垫纸及杯垫）。

任务八　发放餐谱、酒水单

将餐谱/酒水单置于小臂内侧，低于肘关节位；封面对着旅客，将餐谱/酒水单打开至所提供的相应页递送给旅客（注意餐谱应低于旅客视线），并对配备的主菜做简单介绍。

远程线（第一餐）餐饮预定结束后，原则上应将餐谱/酒水单留给旅客浏览，待最后一餐结束后收回。

任务九　订餐

乘务员熟练掌握餐谱内各道餐的中英文名称，主动向旅客介绍；征询旅客对于西式肉类的烹饪需求；主动推荐与旅客所选餐食相匹配的酒类。

VIP 旅客和高端旅客可优先预选餐饮。

对于正在休息或有特殊要求的旅客，应做好记录，并与同舱位的乘务员做好沟通。

在地面未完成的预选可在平飞后继续。

项目四

头等舱餐饮服务标准（空中）

任务一　饮料及餐具准备——正餐/简餐

起飞后及时打开烧水箱(咖啡滴滤烧水壶)、保温箱和冰酒柜。

根据订餐情况，将中西式汤碗放入微波炉内加温(无微波炉的用热水加温)，注意中式汤碗盖无须加热。

根据订餐单，准备冷热饮。

准备餐前饮小推车，所有托盘和抽屉都垫上垫盘纸，餐车及小推车垫上垫车布。

车上层抽屉：各类酒水饮料、热饮壶、咖啡壶、柠檬片、冰桶、冰夹、奶球、搅拌棒、小勺、糖包、胡椒盐(放置在冷饮杯中)。

车下层抽屉：冷、热饮杯，餐桌布(分开叠好、平整干净，餐桌布数量须大于旅客人数，注意餐桌布的正反面：光边为正面)，果仁，餐巾纸。

任务二　饮料及餐具准备——早餐

准备餐前饮小推车。

一般情况下，旅客人数少于20人时，不使用餐车收/发餐食。

所有托盘和抽屉都垫上垫盘纸，餐车及小推车垫上垫车布。

车上层抽屉：各类酒水饮料、热饮壶、咖啡壶、柠檬片、冰桶、冰夹、奶球、搅拌棒、小勺、糖包、胡椒盐(放置在冷饮杯中)。

车下层抽屉：冷、热饮杯，餐桌布(分开叠好、平整干净，餐桌布数量须大于旅客人数，注意餐桌布的正反面：光边为正面)，餐巾纸。

任务三　饮料及餐具准备——快餐

准备餐桌布、刀叉。

根据预选饮料准备相应饮料杯。

任务四　餐食准备——正餐/简餐

根据订餐情况及旅客需求，烤制餐食、中式汤料、面包(蒜蓉面包需打开包装纸）。注意：西式汤料（如：奶油花）无须烤制。

准备开胃小菜（canape），揭开保鲜膜。

揭开冷盘保鲜膜。

准备餐车，根据订餐情况，适当调整中西式冷盘比例，供两边过道同时发放。

清空餐车最上两层，以摆放托盘或盛放汤碗的抽屉。

取出保温壶，根据订餐选择，准备中西式汤，中式汤倒入前，应先放入烤制后的汤料。

一般情况下，旅客人数少于20人时，不使用餐车收/发餐食。

任务五　餐食准备——早餐

根据订餐情况及旅客需求，烤制餐食，用烤箱余温温热早餐面包。预热中式粥碗。将西式麦片装入西式汤碗后放入西式餐盘内。

任务六　餐食准备——快餐

烤制餐食（粥和中式热点）。预热中式粥碗。

任务七　餐食烤制注意事项

✤有预选功能烤箱

鱼类烤制：

经烤制后鱼类在翻盘过程中易碎，应使用面包夹小心移出，使其外观保持完整、美观。如白色鱼肉烤制后有水分析出，应在装盘时去除汤汁（汤汁容易有鱼腥味）。

肉类烤制：

·牛排、羊排类应用高温或烤箱 beef/veal 模式烤制。

·鸡肉（鸡胸）由于肉质较厚，应放置于烤箱中上层或用烤箱 chicken 模式烤制。

·猪肉普遍采用中式料理法，搭配米饭或者面条，应用烤箱 rice/noodles 模式烤制。

蔬菜烤制：

·应确定餐食内蔬菜是否需要烤制，如意大利千层面中的罗勒叶作点缀用，无须加热。

·绿色蔬菜应即烤即食，避免重复加热。

·蔬菜在烤制后有水分析出，应在装盘时去除汤汁。

中式早餐烤制：应置于烤箱中下层，使用 snack 模式烤制，同时应将烤箱提前预热 3～5 分钟，避免点心过焦或过干。

西式早餐烤制：应使用烤箱 egg dish 模式烤制，避免高温或烤制时间过长。

✤ 无预选功能烤箱

一般热食在 180℃下烤制 20 分钟。

牛排或羊排，根据旅客喜好烤制：

·嫩（三成熟）：中温 15 分钟。

·中（五成熟）：中温 20 分钟。

·老（七成熟）：中温 25 分钟。

素食热食在 180℃下烤制 12～15 分钟，烤制完毕后，可重复开/关烤箱若干次散热，以确保餐食色泽鲜艳。

任务八　面包烤制注意事项

✤ 有预选功能烤箱

应使用烤箱 bread 模式烤制，正常情况进行 2 次循环，每次 6 分钟。

蒜蓉面包应从塑料袋中取出，半打开锡纸并置于烤箱上层进行烤制。

早餐面包应敞开塑料袋口，平铺在烤盘上，用烤箱余温或 bread 模式烤制 1 次。

✤ 无预选功能烤箱

正餐面包在 180℃下烤制 10 分钟。

蒜蓉面包须打开包装纸烤制，在 180℃下烤制 12 分钟。

早餐面包在 180℃下烤制 5 分钟。

可颂面包（croissant）用烤制热食后的余温加热。

任务九　铺桌布、提供餐前饮（和果仁）

使用小推车为旅客铺餐桌布、提供餐前饮等。

餐桌布准备工作：

·将餐桌布整理平整、确保清洁。

·餐桌布预备数须大于实际需求数。

·注意确认餐桌布的正反（光边为正面）。

铺餐桌布方法一：

将餐桌布悬挂于手臂。协助旅客打开餐桌。轻轻拉开餐桌布边缘。由桌板过道侧外沿向内展开铺平。轻拉餐布四角以确保餐布平整，不得用手抚平餐布。

铺餐桌布方法二：

轻捏餐桌布两角在餐桌后侧将餐桌布展开。将餐桌布贴和桌面拉向旅客方向铺平。轻拉餐桌布四角以确保餐布平整，不得用手抚平餐桌布。铺餐桌布、餐巾纸、斟倒餐前饮整套程序连贯完成。

任务十　侍酒服务

只要旅客选择葡萄酒则乘务员要提供侍酒服务。

适时向客人推荐与其主菜搭配的葡萄酒。

搭配原则：

食物与葡萄酒的口味轻重相符。

食物的浓郁度和葡萄酒体相符。

用甜的葡萄酒搭配搭配较甜的食物。

用高酸度的酒搭配酸性的食物。

高单宁，也就是较涩的葡萄酒（赤霞珠 Cabernet Sauvigon 或西拉 Syrah/Shiraz），应该搭配筋道的肉类（牛排、羊排等）。

低单宁，不是非常强劲的葡萄酒（美乐 Merlot），适合搭配禽肉类食物（鸡鸭类）。

白葡萄酒适合搭配具有鲜味的食物（如海鲜和鱼类）。

浓郁的芝士宜搭配红葡萄酒，较清淡的芝士（如金文饼等）宜搭配白葡萄酒。

为客人侍酒时应遵循验、开、试、斟、添的原则。

为旅客开酒前应先将酒标正对旅客，并向旅客介绍该款葡萄酒的品牌、产地及年份等。

试酒时，只需为旅客倒一小口葡萄酒的量，如旅客满意再为其斟酒。

试酒时，应先为同行的男性旅客倒酒；但斟酒时，应先为同座的女性旅客倒酒。

更换酒的品种时，必须要更换酒杯。

葡萄酒在斟酒时可以将酒杯放在小桌板的杯槽内倒酒，也可以左手拿住杯脚下1/3倒酒。

为旅客提供葡萄酒服务时还应提供一杯矿泉水。

任务十一　提供 CANAPE

使用托盘为旅客提供餐前小食（canape）。

收回餐前小食（canape）碟时，及时整理旅客餐桌。

任务十二　送冷盘、汤

将放置饮料和杯子的抽屉从饮料车移至餐车上。

使用餐车提供冷盘、汤。

将汤碗放入相应餐盘内，整理后合盘送出。

提供给旅客时，先介绍中西式冷盘及汤的名称（中式汤碗盖当着旅客面打开并带回）。

无法放入餐车的汤，由内场乘务员使用大托盘及时补给。

任务十三　送面包

将烤制后的正餐面包放入已铺好垫布的面包篮，蒜蓉面包须与其他面包隔开，避免串味。

送面包时，适时介绍面包种类。

使用面包夹为旅客提供面包。

送早餐面包时，将大托盘用白色餐布铺好，将早餐面包有序摆放好，确保面包形状饱满。

任务十四　送主菜

送主菜前，及时收回冷荤碟和汤碗（提醒旅客稍后提供主菜）。

热食摆盘原则：先摆放淀粉类主食，再摆放配菜（颜色交错搭配），再摆放主菜，最后浇汁。

在公务舱旅客人数较多的情况下，可酌情预摆盘（牛排等除外），浇汁与热食一并放入烤箱保温，送出前方可浇汁，浇汁不宜过多，浇汁量以刚好能从主食上滴下为宜。

用托盘提供中式热主食时需饭菜分离，可带上备份刀叉。

及时添加热面包。

合盘收回所有用完的餐具、杯子（可视旅客用餐情况，使用餐车收取用具）。

任务十五　送芝士和水果

用小推车摆放芝士、水果后送出。

芝士服务标准

揭开芝士盘内所有食材的保鲜膜，分摘成串的葡萄。

芝士盘内准备：冰夹、刀、叉（每种芝士各一把刀、叉）。

小推车上层：沙拉碟、刀叉包、餐巾纸、红酒、矿泉水、酒杯、长饮杯若干。

小推车下层：份装水果。

向旅客展示芝士，并介绍芝士品种、产地、口味，同时介绍可搭配的葡萄酒，先询问芝士需求再提供水果。

芝士装盘要摆放美观、整洁：一种芝士使用一把刀切割，用叉子辅助；葡萄等配料使用冰夹拿取，放入盘内。芝士摆盘原则：饼干或面包干垫放于芝士下；各种辅料和芝士搭配立体，色彩分明；不同芝士不应混放在一起，避免窜味；芝士尖角不能对着旅客。

及时介绍并提供葡萄酒侍酒服务。

水果服务标准

水果摆盘原则：尽量各种水果全部呈现；色彩搭配明朗；如果旅客有特殊需求，可对水果摆盘做调整。

提供早餐水果时，可将水果盘和干净刀叉放入餐车内最上层，收回旅客餐盘的同时送上水果。

先放餐具再提供芝士和水果，并将餐巾纸放在旅客右手下方。

任务十六　送甜品、热饮

用小推车准备甜品和热饮，根据旅客需要提供热饮。

小推车上层：蛋糕、冰激凌、餐巾纸、热饮壶、奶球、叉子、小勺、糖包。

小推车下层：热饮杯、杯托、备用蛋糕/冰激凌。

提供服务时，先放餐具，再放蛋糕/冰激凌，最后放热饮，将餐巾纸放在旅客右手下方。

咖啡和茶送出时，必须是烫的。

茶/咖啡匙置于杯碟上，杯把和茶匙摆放在同一侧（旅客的右手侧）。

任务十七　送巧克力、餐后酒

小推车提供巧克力、餐后酒（白兰地、力娇酒等）。

小推车上层：巧克力、餐后酒、古典杯、白兰地杯、餐巾纸、冰桶、冰夹。

小推车下层：大托盘、空抽屉（供外场收回甜品盘和餐具）。

主动向旅客介绍机上餐后酒品种和产地，根据其需求提供餐后酒服务。

提供力娇酒时应使用古典杯，并加入碎冰。

先放置餐后酒，再放置巧克力。

收回甜品盘及其他的餐具，应放于小推车下层。

任务十八　送快餐

用手托的方式送快餐。

中式快餐：将中式热点、佐菜一同置于热食盘上，配上粥和刀叉包，一并放于旅客餐桌上。

西式快餐：将西式快餐碟和刀叉包逐一放于旅客餐桌上。

任务十九　送早餐

用手托的方式提供餐盘。

中式早餐：餐盘内放入中式热食、粥，合盘托出。

西式早餐：餐盘内放入西式热食；送出前，在麦片碗内倒入牛奶，合盘托出。

日式早餐：将汤料放在碗内，开水冲泡；餐盘内放入日式热食、汤、小菜，合盘托出。

任务二十　收回餐具

观察、识别或询问旅客是否已用餐完毕，主动询问旅客对餐食的反馈及是否需要添加冷热饮。

将餐具适当整理，摆放整齐，防止汤汁外溢，避免发出响声。

回收餐布时，应根据由内向外原则将餐桌布折叠好，垫于托盘下；旅客主动递上时，应尽快收回并表示感谢。

第二部分

乘务员播音艺术

Task 1　Check-in and Departure

Learning Objective

Knowledge Objectives

1. To know how to make an announcement about check-in and departure.

2. To learn some useful expressions about check-in and departure.

Skill Objectives

1. To master to make an announcement about check-in and departure.

2. To master to deal with check-in effectively and rightly.

Quality Objectives

1. To develop the sense of responsibility.

2. To be knowledgeable and professional.

Part Ⅰ　Lead-in

Questions：

1. Have you ever heard of any announcements at the airport? What time should the passengers get to the airport?

2. Before the flight, passengers need to know the aircraft type and flight time. Therefore, airport announcement is very important. It helps to establish the basis of communication and ensure a safe and pleasurable flight.

Part Ⅱ　Reading

1. Ladies and gentlemen, may I have your attention please? We're now ready for check-in for Flight No. 3576 to New York at counter No. 12. Thank you.

女士们，先生们，请注意。我们现在准备在 12 号柜台办理飞往纽约的 3576 号航班的登机手续。谢谢。

2. Ladies and gentlemen, may I have your attention please? Passengers for Flight No. 6987 to Tokyo who have not checked-in for this flight, please go to the counter immediately.

女士们，先生们，请注意。尚未办理飞往东京的 6987 号航班登机手续的乘客，请立即前往柜台。

3. Passengers taking Flight No. 9947 to Beijing, attention please. Please go to the counter No. 37 to exchange your boarding passes for transit passes. Thank you.

搭乘 9947 航班飞往北京的乘客，请注意。请前往 37 号柜台，将您的登机牌换成过境证。谢谢！

4. Ladies and gentlemen, may I have your attention please? Stand by passengers for Flight No. 1754 to Hangzhou, please go to counter No. 25 for check-in.

女士们，先生们，请注意。前往杭州的 1754 号航班的候补乘客，请前往 25 号柜台办理登机手续。

Part Ⅲ　Words and Expressions

1. announce [ə'naʊns]　v. 宣布；预示；播报
   announcement [ə'naʊnsmənt]　n. 通知，公告
   make an announcement　发布通知
   cabin announcement　客舱广播
2. ready ['redi]　adj. 准备好的，现成的
   to be ready for sth(prepared for)　为……做好准备
   to get ready for　为……做准备，强调准备的动作
3. passenger ['pæsɪndʒə(r)]　n. 旅客，乘客
4. check-in　到达并登记；报到；值机
5. proceed to　去往某地；开始，着手
6. due to(because of)　因为，由于(作副词，表原因)

Part Ⅳ　Reading Skill

连读

连读就是在英语交流中，使用较快语速时，相邻的两词所发生的类似单词连音拼读的语音现象。两词连读一般应具备以下条件：相邻两词在意义上必须密切相关，同属一个意群。

连读构成的音节一般不重读，只需顺其自然地一带而过，不可读得太重。连读主要出现在意义联系较紧的词，如冠词与名词、数词与名词、动词与副词、连接词与代名词之间。

语意自然停顿的地方，即有逗号、句号等标点符号的地方，不用连读。英语中常见的连读现象主要以下有几种。

1. "辅音+元音"型连读
在同一个意群里，如果相邻两词中的前一个词是以辅音结尾，后一个词是以元

音开头，这就要将辅音与元音拼起来连读。

I'm ~ an ~ English boy.

It ~ is ~ an ~ old book.

Let me have ~ a look ~ at ~ it.

Ms Black worked in ~ an ~ office last ~ yesterday.

I called ~ you half ~ an ~ hour ~ ago.

2. "r/re+元音" 型连读

如果前一个词是以-r 或者-re 结尾，后一个词是以元音开头，这时的 r 或 re 不但要发/r/，而且还要与后面的元音拼起来连读。

They're my father ~ and mother.

I looked for ~ it here ~ and there.

There ~ is a football under ~ it.

There ~ are some books on the desk.

Here ~ is a letter for you.

Here ~ are four ~ eggs.

But where ~ is my cup?

Where ~ are your brother ~ and sister?

但是，如果一个音节的前后都有字母 r，即使后面的词以元音开头，也不能连读。

The black clouds are coming nearer and nearer. (nearer 与 and 不可连读)

3. "辅音+半元音" 型连读

英语语音中的/j/和/w/是半元音，如果前一个词是以辅音结尾，后一个词是以半元音，特别是/j/开头，此时也要连读。

Thank ~ you.

Nice to meet ~ you.

Did ~ you get there late ~ again?

Would ~ you like ~ a cup ~ of tea?

Could ~ you help me, please?

"音的同化" —常把/d/+/j/读成/dV/，did you 听上成了/dɪdVu/，would you 成了/wudVu/，could you 成了/kudVu/.

4. "元音+元音" 型连读

连读如果前一个词以元音结尾，后一个词以元音开头，这两个音往往也要自然而不间断地连读到一起.

I ~ am Chinese.

He ~ is very friendly to me.

She wants to study ~ English.

How ~ and why did you come here?

She can't carry ~ it.

It will take you three ~ hours to walk there.

The question is too ~ easy for him to answer.

Part V　Practical Practices

1. Match the expressions in Column A with their Chinese equivalents in Column B.

Column A		Column B	
(1)	bound for	A	通过
(2)	formality	B	值机柜台
(3)	proceed	C	柜台
(4)	check-in counter	D	立即，马上
(5)	go through	E	合作
(6)	cooperation	F	随身物品，所有物
(7)	immediately	G	开始行动，继续做
(8)	belongings	H	飞往……
(9)	counter	I	旅客
(10)	passenger	J	正式手续

2. Translate the following sentences into English.

（1）请乘坐此次航班的旅客，拿好随身物品，到 1 号柜台办理登机手续。

（2）还未办理登机手续的旅客，请尽快到值机柜台办理。

（3）CA1234 次航班将在 30 分钟后起飞。

（4）飞往上海的 CA1234 次航班，即将在 20 分钟后办完登机手续。

（5）女士们，先生们，飞往上海的 CA1234 次航班，现在开始办理登机手续。

（6）CA1234 次航班的登机口号码已由 8 号改为 9 号。

3. Translate the following sentences into Chinese.

（1）Passengers for this flight please board through Gate No. 12.

（2）We hope you will enjoy your flight.

（3）We apologize for the inconvenience.

（4）This is the final call for passengers traveling to Shanghai.

（5）May I have your attention, please?

（6）Please refrain from smoking beyond the gate.

4. Oral English practice

（1）Thank you for waiting, Ladies and gentlemen,

Flight _____ for _____ is now ready for boarding. Will passengers on this flight please make their way to Gate _____ . Please refrain from smoking beyond the gate. Thank you.

（2）Attention please.

This is the final call for passengers traveling to _____ . _____ is now boarding. Passengers are kindly requested to proceed to Gate _____ . Thank you.

（3）Ladies and gentlemen,

May I have your attention please? Check-in counters for Flight _____ bound for _____ will be closed in half an hour. Passengers who have not done check-in formalities, please go to the check-in counters immediately.

We hope you will enjoy your flight with _____ (airlines).

Thank you.

Task 2　Notice of Flight Cancellation

Knowledge Objectives

1. To know how to make an announcement about flight cancellation.

2. To learn some useful expressions about notice of flight cancellation.

Skill Objectives

1. To be able to make an announcement about flight cancellation.

2. To master a reading skill.

Quality Objectives

1. To develop the sense of responsibility.

2. To be knowledgeable and professional.

Part Ⅰ　Lead-in

Question：

Do you know how to announce flight delay? Have you ever listen to the delay announcements at the airport?

There are many reasons of delays.

1. Weather　天气

2. Air Traffic Control　空中管制

3. Airports Reasons　机场原因

5. Passengers Reasons　旅客原因

4. Airlines Reasons　航空公司原因

Part Ⅱ　Reading

航班取消通知（进港类）

Ladies and gentlemen, may I have your attention please?

We regret to announce that（Zhongyuan Airlines）Flight NB5128 from Guiyang has been cancelled due to:

the poor weather condition at our airport;

the poor weather condition over the air route;

the poor weather condition at Guiyang airport;

aircraft reallocation;

the maintenance of the aircraft;

the aircraft maintenance at Guiyang airport;

air traffic congestion;

the close-down of Guiyang airport;

communication trouble.

This flight has been rescheduled to tomorrow at 13:40.

Thank you.

女士们先生们，请注意：

我们抱歉地通知，由贵阳飞来本站的（中原航空）NB5128 次航班取消了，由于：

本机场天气不够飞行标准；

航路天气不够飞行标准；

贵阳机场天气不够飞行标准；

飞机调配原因；

飞机机械原因；

飞机在贵阳机场出现机械故障；

航行管制原因；

贵阳机场关闭；

通信原因。

本航班将改期至明日 13 时 40 分，谢谢！

Part Ⅲ　Words and Expressions

1. cancel［ˈkæns(ə)l］ *v.* 删去，划掉；勾销，盖销（邮票等）；取消，废除，中止

2. aircraft reallocation　飞机调配

　　reallocation［riːˌælə'keɪʃn］　调配；再分配

3. the maintenance of the aircraft　飞机机械原因

　　maintain［meɪn'teɪn］ *v.* 保持；维持；继续供养；扶养维修，保养（机器、道路等）；坚持，维护

　　maintain a highway　保养公路

　　maintenance［ˈmeɪntənəns］ *n.* 保持、维持；维护

　　maintain one's family　供养家庭

4. air traffic congestion   航空管制

（traffic congestion 比较偏向"交通拥挤"的意思；而 traffic jam 则是说"交通阻塞"。）

Part Ⅳ   Reading Skill

语音语调——升调

升调多用来表示"不肯定"和"未完结"的意思，如一般疑问句，语气婉转的祈使句，以及用陈述句子形式表示疑问的各类句子。例如：

1. Shall I tell him to come and see you? 用于一般疑问句表示正常语调。

2. You like him? 用于陈述句形式的疑问句中，期待得到对方证实。

3. What have you got there? 用于特殊疑问句中，语气亲切热情。

4. Right you are. 用于某些感叹句中，表示轻快、活泼、鼓励等意义。

5. She bought red, yellow and green rugs. 用于排比句中，区别语义。

Part Ⅴ   Practical Practices

1. Match the expressions in Column A with their Chinese equivalents in Column B.

Column A		Column B	
（1） attention	A	由于；应归于
（2） reallocation	B	再分配
（3） maintain	C	取消
（4） inconvenience	D	航班
（5） due to	E	道歉
（6） apologize	F	延误
（7） cancel	G	拥挤
（8） congestion	H	不便
（9） flight	I	保养，维护
（10） delay	J	注意

2. Translate the following sentences into English.

（1）感谢您的合作。

（2）我们抱歉地通知，您乘坐的航班，由于天气原因，决定取消今日飞行。

（3）对于给各位带来的不便，我们深表歉意。

3. Translate the following sentences into Chinese.

（1）Flight CA1234 to Shanghai has been canceled because of weather conditions at local airport.

（2）We regret to announce that flight CA1234 from Guiyang has been canceled due to air traffic congestion.

（3）This flight has been rescheduled to tomorrow at 13：40.

4. Oral English practice

（1）Ladies and gentlemen,

Please remain seated while we are waiting for（some passengers/ transit passengers）to get on board.

Thank you for your understanding!

（2）Ladies and gentlemen,

As more food will be sent to the aircraft for the occasion, there will be a short delay for a few minutes.

Thank you for your understanding!

（3）Ladies and gentlemen,

As the loading documents have not been sent to the aircraft, there will be a delay for a few minutes.

Thank you for your understanding!

（5）Ladies and gentlemen,

I'm sorry to have to inform you that operational requirements have made it necessary for us to transfer to another aircraft. Please disembark with all your personal effects and follow our ground staff to the new aircraft. We apologize for the inconvenience.

Thank you for your cooperation!

Task 3　Baggage Arrangement

Knowledge Objectives

1. To know how to make an announcement about baggage arrangement.

2. To learn some useful expressions about arranging baggage.

Skill Objectives

1. To be able to master the keywords and expressions.

2. To master a reading skill.

Quality Objectives

1. To develop the serious work attitude and the sense of responsibility.

2. To be knowledgeable and professional.

Part Ⅰ　Lead-in

Questions：

1. Where can passengers know the seat number?

2. If you can not find your seat, what can you do?

3. How to help passengers arrange their baggage in the cabin?

4. How to arrange seats for passengers in the cabin?

Part Ⅱ　Reading

Baggage Arrangement

Ladies and gentlemen,

Welcome aboard ＿＿＿＿＿＿ Airlines. Please take your seat according to your seat number. Your seat number is on the edge of the rack. Please make sure your hand baggage is stored in the overhead locker. Any small articles can be put under the seat in front of you. Please take your seat as soon as possible to keep the aisle clear for others to go through.

Thank you!

引导入座广播

各位女士，各位先生：

欢迎您搭乘_____航空公司的班机，请您对照手中登机牌上的号码对号入座，座位号位于行李架边缘。大件行李请放在行李架上，并请放置稳妥整齐；小件物品建议您放在您前排座椅下方。请尽快入座，保持过道畅通以方便其他旅客顺利通过。谢谢！

Part Ⅲ Words and Expressions

1. welcome aboard 请上船（或车、飞机）
2. the edge 边缘
3. baggage〔ˈbæɡɪdʒ〕 *n.* 行李
4. luggage〔ˈlʌɡɪdʒ〕 *n.* 行李

luggage 和 baggage 两者都表示"行李"，均是不可数名词。luggage 属英式英语，是随身携带行李的总称；baggage 属美式英语，是各种行李的总称。当询问行李的数量时，用 how much 引导疑问句；指行李的件数，需与 a piece of 或 an article of 连用。例如：

two pieces of luggage/baggage 两件行李

three articles of luggage/baggage 三件行李

5. overhead〔ˌəʊvəˈhed〕 *adv.* 在头顶上；在空中；在高处

Part Ⅳ Reading Skill

采用正确的广播语速

正常情况下的客舱广播无论使用中文还是英文，注意放慢语速、放缓语气。科学表明，理想的播音速度是每分钟 240 至 250 字，这符合人耳对熟悉语言的接受和辨析习惯。我们可以将自己的广播进行录音回放，换位思考一下第一次乘坐飞机的旅客能否听清，并且有意识地计算记忆的时间。

Part V Practical Practices

1. Match the expressions in Column A with their Chinese equivalents in Column B.

Column A		Column B	
（1） article	A	边缘
（2） edge	B	行李
（3） baggage	C	物品
（4） locker	D	储物架
（5） aisle	E	过道

2. Translate the following sentences into English.

（1）座位号位于行李架边缘。

（2）小件物品建议您放在您前排座椅下方。

（3）欢迎您乘坐东方航空公司的班机。

3. Translate the following sentences into Chinese.

（1）Please take your seat according to your seat number.

（2）Please take your seat as soon as possible to keep the aisle clear for others to go through.

（3）Please make sure your hand baggage is stored in the overhead locker.

4. Oral English practice

（1）Ladies and gentlemen,

Welcome aboard flight CA1234 from Tianjin to Guangzhou. Would you please check your ticket and boarding pass again to make sure you're boarding the right flight?

As you enter the cabin, we kindly ask you that take your seat as soon as possible to give room for other passengers who may be standing in the aisle behind you.

Your seat number is indicated on the bottom edge of the overhead baggage compartment. Please place your carry-on baggage in the overhead compartment.

Small or fragile baggage should be placed under the seat in front of you.

Please do not leave any baggage either in the aisle or near an exit door.

Thank you for your cooperation!

（2）Ladies and gentlemen,

We must keep the balance of the aircraft, so please take your seat according to your seat number.

Thank you for your cooperation!

Task 4　Boarding

Learning Objective

Knowledge Objectives

1. To know how to make an announcement about boarding.

2. To learn some useful expressions about boarding.

3. To know the keywords and expressions on board.

Skill Objectives

1. To master a reading skill.

Quality Objectives

1. To familiarize with the work flow of boarding and develop the sense of responsibility.

2. To be knowledgeable and professional.

Part Ⅰ　Lead-in

Question：

How to greet the passengers when they are boarding?

Part Ⅱ　Reading

Ladies and gentlemen，good morning（afternoon/evening）.

Welcome aboard China Southern Airlines flight CZ5239，from Shanghai to New York. Our plane will be taking off immediately. Please fasten your seat belt，make sure your seat back is straight up and your tray table is closed. The purser with all cabin crew members will be sincere at your service. We hope you enjoy the flight! Thank you!

女士们先生们，早上（下午/晚上）好：

欢迎乘坐南方航空公司从上海飞往纽约的 CZ5239 次航班。我们的飞机马上要起飞了，请您系好安全带，调直座椅靠背，收起小桌板。乘务长携全体机组人员竭诚为您服务。希望您旅途愉快！谢谢！

Part Ⅲ　Words and Expressions

1. cabin crew（CA）/flight attendant　乘务员，乘务长，空姐，空乘，空中乘务员

2. seat number　座位号

seat by number　对号入座

3. boarding card/pass　登机牌

boarding pass 和 board-pass 都指登机牌，而 boarding pass 除了指登机牌之外，还有其他意思。也就是一般用 board-pass 指登机牌的时候多。

4. fasten［ˈfɑːsn］　*vt.* 系牢，钉牢；使坚固或稳固

　　　　　　　　　　vi. 附着，扣紧；紧握，紧抱；集中

5. seatbelt［siːtbelt］　*n.* 安全带

6. fasten your seat belt　系好安全带

fasten on/upon　集中于……；集中注意力于……

Part Ⅳ　Reading Skill

语音语调——降调

降调表示"肯定"和"完结"，一般用于陈述句、特殊疑问句、命令句和感叹句中。具体见以下 5 个句子。

1. 用于陈述句表示肯定的意义。

eg. Swimming is my favorite ∈ sport.

2. 用于特殊疑问句表示说话人浓厚的兴趣。

eg. What did you find ∈ there?

3. 表示语气较强的命令。

eg. Tell me all about ∈ it.

4. 用于一般疑问句表示说话人的态度粗率、不耐烦或不高兴。

eg. Have you got the ∈ tickets?

5. 用于感叹句，表示感叹。

eg. How ∈ nice!

英语中除了升调、降调这两种最基本的语调外，还有降—升调、升—降调、升—降—升调、平调等。我们掌握了基本的降升调后，可以增加阅读量以提高语感。

Part Ⅴ　Practical Practices

1. Match the expressions in Column A with their Chinese equivalents in Column B.

Column A		Column B	
（1）	stewardess	A	正确的
（2）	seatbelt	B	空姐
（3）	flight	C	安全带
（4）	check	D	检查
（5）	correct	E	航班

2. Translate the following sentences into English.

(1)欢迎乘坐中国国际航空公司从天津飞往广州的 CA1234 次航班。

(2)希望您旅途愉快。

3. Translate the following sentences into Chinese.

(1)Would you please check your ticket and boarding pass again to make sure you're boarding the correct flight.

(2)The purser with all cabin crew members will be sincere at your service.

4. Oral English practice

Ladies and gentlemen,

Now the plane will be taking off and the flight attendants will do safety check. Please fasten your seatbelts, stow your tray table, return your footrest to its initial position and put your seat back to the upright position. Please help us by opening the sunshades. Your cooperation will be appreciated.

Thank you.

Task 5　Welcome Speech

Learning Objective

Knowledge Objectives

1. To know how to make a welcome speech.

2. To learn some useful expressions about speech of welcome.

Skill Objectives

1. To be able to use the keywords and the expressions.

2. To master a reading skill.

Quality Objectives

1. To cultivate a sense of service responsibility.

2. To be knowledgeable and professional.

Part Ⅰ　Lead-in

Questions：

1. How to greet the passengers when they are boarding?

2. How to help passengers arrange their baggage in the cabin?

3. How to arrange seats for passengers in the cabin?

4. When passengers are boarding the airplane, flight attendants are standing in their own designated areas to welcome the passengers.

Part Ⅱ　Reading

Good morning, ladies and gentlemen,

Welcome aboard Air China flight CA4117/Chengdu to Beijing (via Xi'an). The distance between Chengdu and Beijing is 1 982 kilometers. Our flight will take 3 hours and 35 minutes. We will be flying at the altitude of 10 000 meters and the average speed is 800 kilometers per hour.

In order to ensure the normal operation of aircraft navigation and communication systems, telephones, laptop computers and other electronic devices throughout the flight are not allowed to use during take-off and landing.

We will take off soon. Please make sure that your seat belt is securely fastened and that you refrain from smoking during the flight.

On our flight today, the chief purser with all the crew members will be sincerely at your service. We hope you will enjoy your flight. Thank you!

女士们，先生们，早上好！

欢迎您乘坐中国航空公司由成都飞往北京（途径西安）的 CA4117 次航班。由成都至北京的飞行距离是 1 982 公里，预计空中飞行时间是 3 小时 35 分。飞行高度 10 000 米，飞行速度平均速度每小时 800 公里。为了保障飞机导航及通信系统的正常工作，在飞机起飞和下降过程中请不要使用手提电话、手提式电脑和其他电子设备。

飞机很快就要起飞了，请您系好安全带，在整个旅途中请不要吸烟。

本次航班的乘务长协同机上其他乘务员竭诚为您提供及时周到的服务。谢谢！

Part Ⅲ　Words and Expressions

1. via ['vaɪə]　*prep.* 取道，通过；经由
2. altitude ['æltɪtjuːd]　*n.* 高度，海拔；飞行高度
3. average ['ævərɪdʒ]　*adj.* 平均的；普通的
   average speed　平均速度
4. normal operation ['nɔːm(ə)l][ˌɒpə'reɪʃ(ə)n]　*n.* 常规操作
5. navigation [ˌnævɪ'ɡeɪʃ(ə)n]　*n.* 导航，领航
6. communication [kəˌmjuːnɪ'keɪʃ(ə)n]　*n.* 交流，交际，通信
7. system ['sɪstəm]　*n.* 系统
8. electronic [ɪˌlek'trɒnɪk]　*adj.* 电子的；电动的
9. device [dɪ'vaɪs]　*n.* 装置；设备
   electronic device　电子设备
10. refrain [rɪ'freɪn]　*vi.* 制止；避免；节制；克制；忍住

Part Ⅳ　Reading Skill

关于飞行距离、飞行时间和代码共享等航线信息的朗读技巧

广播短句建议依据广播词字符之间的空格来断句。如：我谨代表全体机组/欢迎您搭乘/天合联盟成员/中国东方航空班机/前往＿＿＿＿。

相邻两个词，前者以辅音音素结尾，后者以元音音素开头，往往要拼在一起连读。

eg. 1 小时 40 分钟　　one hour and fourty minutes

因此 one hour 读法为 ［wʌn aʊr］

每次练习，带着重点，比如第一次关注连贯，第二次关注停顿，第三次关注音调等，并要对比自己与原声差别，逐步改进。高质量的客舱广播是航空公司服务质量和管理水平的直接体现。

Part V Practical Practices

1. Match the expressions in Column A with their Chinese equivalents in Column B.

	Column A		Column B
（1）	electronic	A	系统
（2）	navigation	B	导航
（3）	device	C	高度
（4）	altitude	D	设备
（5）	system	E	电子的

2. Translate the following sentences into English.

（1）我们的飞行高度为 10 000 米，飞行平均速度为每小时 800 千米。

（2）请您系好安全带，在整个旅途中请不要吸烟。

3. Translate the following sentences into Chinese.

（1）On our flight today, the chief purser with all the crew members will be sincere at your service.

（2）In order to ensure the normal operation of aircraft navigation and communication systems, laptop computers are not allowed to use during take-off and landing.

4. Oral English Practice

Ladies and gentlemen,

May I have your attention, please? Welcome aboard Hainan Airlines, Flight HU7607. We are bound for Beijing on a Boeing 767 and the flight time is about 2 hours and 10 minutes. Please take your seat according to your seat number. Your hand baggage can be put in the overhead compartment or under the seat in front of you. Please don't put anything in the emergency exits. If you need any assistance, please contact our flight attendants. We will land in Beijing Capital International Airport Terminal 3.

Thank you!

Task 6　Flight Route Introduction

Knowledge Objectives

1. To know how to make an introduction about flight route.

2. To learn some useful expressions about flight route.

Skill Objectives

1. To know keywords and expressions.

2. To master a reading skill.

Quality Objectives

1. To cultivate a rigorous and serious work attitude.

2. To be knowledgeable and professional.

Part Ⅰ　Lead-in

Questions：

1. How do the cabin attendant greet passengers?

2. What contents does the pre-flight briefing consist of?

Part Ⅱ　Reading

Ladies and gentlemen，

Welcome your aboard China Southern Airlines flight CZ6887.

We have left Wulumuqi for Guangzhou. The distance between Wulumuqi and Guangzhou is 3373 kilometers. Our flight will take 4 hours and 15 minutes，we expect to arrive at Guangzhou Baiyum International Airport at 14：20 PM.

Along this route，we will be flying over the provinces of Xinjiang，Gansu，Sichuan，Guizhou，Guangxi and Guangdong，acrossing over the Tianshan，QiLianshan，Changjiang River and Zhujiang River.

For your safety，we strongly recommend you to keep your seat belt fastened at all times，as there may be unexpected turbulence in flight.

Lunch and beverages have been prepared for you. If you need any assistance, please feel comfortable to contact any one of us.

We wish you a pleasant journey. Thank you!

女士们，先生们：

欢迎您乘坐中国南方航空公司 CZ6887 次航班。

我们的飞机已经离开乌鲁木齐前往广州，由乌鲁木齐至广州的飞行距离是 3373 千米，飞行时间 4 小时 15 分钟，预计到达广州白云国际机场的时间是 14：20。

沿着这条航线我们将途经新疆、甘肃、四川、贵州、广西、广东，我们还将飞越天山、祁连山、长江、珠江。

在飞行全程中可能会出现因气流变化而引起的突然颠簸，我们特别提醒您，请全程系好安全带。

旅途中，我们为您准备了午餐及各种饮料，如果您需要帮助，我们很乐意随时为您服务。

祝您旅途愉快，谢谢！

Part Ⅲ　Words and Expressions

1. fly over the river　在河面上飞行

fly across the river　飞过那条河

walk over the bridge　走在桥上

walk across the bridge　通过那座桥

2. between... and...　在……和……之间，between 只能表示"在两者之间"，既可以表示时间也可以表示位置。当表示位置时，"在三者或三者以上之间/之中"要用 among。

Part Ⅳ　Reading Skill

省力技巧（略音）：辅音+辅音

略音也被称为省音（也叫不完全爆破），是一种常见的音变现象。在日常谈话中，为了说话时更省力，人们经常把一些音省掉。省音既可以出现在单词内，也可以出现在词与词之间。

在读以［t］［d］［k］［g］［p］开头和以辅音+辅音结尾的单词时，前面的辅音发音顿息，舌头达到发音部位"点到为止"，不送气！在正常速度或快速的对话中，字尾有［t］［d］时通常不会把［t］［d］的发音清楚地念出来，而是快要念出来时，马上憋气顿息，因此字尾［d］［t］的发音常常是听不到的。如示例中的 t，都被省音。

eg. I don't know what to do.

Part Ⅵ Practical Practices

1. Match the expressions in Column A with their Chinese equivalents in Column B.

Column A		Column B	
(1)	distance	A	距离
(2)	assistance	B	建议
(3)	turbulence	C	颠簸
(4)	recommend	D	旅程
(5)	journey	E	协助

2. Translate the following sentences into English.

（1）由天津至上海的飞行距离是 1080 千米。

（2）旅途中，我们为您准备了正餐及各种饮料。

3. Translate the following sentences into Chinese.

（1）For your safety, we strongly recommend you to keep your seat belt fastened at all times, as there may be unexpected turbulence in flight.

（2）If you need any assistance, please feel comfortable to contact any one of us.

4. Oral English practice

（1）Ladies and gentlemen,

We have just left _____ for _____ . During our trip, we shall provide the service of lunch with beverages. We have prepared newspapers and magazines for you. This aircraft has audio system, you can use the earphone and the screen to choose what you like.

Our captain is a pilot with rich flying experiences. His perfect flying skills will ensure you a safe journey. Meanwhile, we have rich working experiences of providing servioes for special passengers. To ensure your safety during the flight, we advise you to fasten your seatbelt while seated. If you have any needs or requirements, please let us know.

Wish you a pleasant journey!

Thank you!

(2) Ladies and gentlemen,

This is your purser speaking. Welcome aboard _____ Airlines.

The plane you are taking is Airbus 320. Now we are going to _____, the whole flight takes about _____ hours _____ minutes. We will be landing at our destination at _____ (time). According to CAAC, to ensure safety, we will provide cabin service 20 minutes after take-off. Today we have prepared lunch and several beverages.

Also we have prepared some nice items for you. Please enjoy your shopping time later. For your convenience of travel, you can get the application forms of _____ Club and comment card from our cabin crew.

We may encounter some turbulence, please fasten your seatbelt when you are seated, and make the seatbelt outside your blanket to avoid being bothered.

We wish you a pleasant journey!

Thank you!

Task 7   Emergency Exit

Learning Objective

Knowledge Objectives

1. To know how to make an announcement about emergency exit.

2. To learn some useful expressions about emergency exit.

Skill Objectives

1. To master the keywords and expressions.

2. To master a reading skill.

Quality Objectives

1. To develop the awareness of security and responsibility.

2. To be knowledgeable and professional.

Part Ⅰ   Lead-in

Question：

How to introduce the Safety Instruction to the passengers sit at the emergency exit?

Part Ⅱ   Reading

Location of emergency exits

Ladies and gentlemen，

Good morning/afternoon/evening.

To be safe we will show you the location of the emergency exits.

There are six/eight/ten emergency exits located at the forward，rear and middle of the cabin.

We will show you safety demonstration video and appreciate your attention.

Thank you！

（广播时机：飞机关门后、插放视频《安全须知》前广播）

各位女生，各位先生：

早上／中午／晚上好！

安全起见，我们将为您介绍紧急出口的位置。

客舱内共有6/8/10个紧急出口，分别位于客舱的前部、后部和中部。

接下来，我们将为您播放安全须知，敬请关注。谢谢！

（注意：无论是在实际飞行中，还是在英语综合能力测试中，用英文介绍飞机的紧急出口都是必不可少的，也是重中之重。

我们来总结一下介绍紧急出口的关键点：

1. 评定该旅客是否可以坐在紧急出口；

2. 向旅客介绍紧急出口使用方法并让其监控；

3. 向旅客说明紧急出口处座位的小桌板的使用方法及对出口行李的要求；

4. 询问旅客是否听懂及是否愿意坐在这里；

5. 如果旅客愿意，请他／她阅读安全须知卡并且向他／她表示感谢；如果旅客不愿意，可帮助他／她调换座位。）

Part Ⅲ Words and Expressions

1. the location of 位置，场所；位置〔地点〕的选定；定位；外景（拍摄地）

   look for the location (for) 寻找（……的）位置

   pinpoint a location 精确地指出位置

   secure the location 确定地点

2. emergency exit 紧急出口

   emergency [ɪˈmɜːdʒənsi] n. 突然事件；紧急情况，非常时期

   exit [ˈeksɪt] n. 出口，通道；vi.（戏剧）退场

3. rear [rɪə(r)] n.（建筑物或车辆等的）后部

Part Ⅳ Reading Skill

对客舱播音的强调处理

进行广播时，不要太情绪化，我们应该用一个正式而权威的声调，通过广播去传达信息。在广播过程中重音强调相关的一些动词名词，如机门、关闭、旅客、就座、离机等。播音时，应咬字清晰，语气亲切，语速自然适中。需要强调某些信息时，可通过重读、高调、延音等方式实现。播音应稳重大方，克服吐字发音的不良习惯，在现有发声条件的基础上发挥长处、克服短处，扩展发声能力，找到自己最好的声音，纠正"压、挤、捏、噎、憋"等错误的用气发声状态。

Part V　Practical Practices

1. Match the expressions in Column A with their Chinese equivalents in Column B.

Column A		Column B	
(1)	location	A	示范、演示
(2)	emergency	B	位置
(3)	rear	C	后部
(4)	exit	D	出口
(5)	demonstration	E	紧急的

2. Translate the following sentences into English.

(1) 现在飞机舱门已经关闭。

(2) 客舱内共有 6 个紧急出口，分别位于客舱的前部、后部和中部。

3. Translate the following sentences into Chinese.

(1) We will show you safety demonstration video and appreciate your attention.

(2) To be safe we will show you the location of the emergency exits.

4. Oral English practice

(1) Ladies and gentlemen,

Now we will inform you the safety instructions. Please pay attention to the presentation. Thank you.

(2) Ladies and gentlemen,

May I have your attention please for the video of safety demonstration? If you have any questions, please contact flight attendants.

Thank you.

(3) Ladies and gentlemen,

Now the flight attendants will tell you the location of your nearest exit. Follow the instructions of the flight attendants and do not take anything while evacuating. If the exit cannot be used, move to another one immediately.

Task 8   Safety Demonstration

Knowledge Objectives

1. To know how to make an announcement about safety demonstration.

2. To learn some useful expressions about safety demonstration.

Skill Objectives

1. To know the keywords and expressions.

2. To master a reading skill.

Quality Objectives

1. To develop the sense of safety awareness.

2. To be knowledgeable and professional.

Part I   Lead-in

Questions:

1. What are the safety demonstration items in the cabin?

2. Do you know how to explain the using-way of safety demonstration items to passengers?

Part II   Reading

Ladies and gentlemen,

Our flight attendants will now demonstrate the use of life vest, oxygen mask and seatbelt, and show you the location of the emergency exits.

Your life vest is placed under your seat. Slip the life-vest over your head.

Bring the waist strap around our waist. Fasten the buckles and tighten it by pulling it outwards.

To inflate your life-vest, pull firmly on the red cord before leaving the aircraft.

To inflate further, blow into these mouthpieces.

Your oxygen mask is placed in a compartment above your seat. It will drop automatically in case of decompression.

Pull the mask down sharply to activate the flow of oxygen.

Place the mask over your nose and mouth. Pull the elastic strap over your head and tighten it by pulling the end of the strap. In a few seconds, the oxygen will begin to flow.

Your seatbelt contains two pieces. To fasten the belt, slip one piece into the buckle and tighten it.

Please keep your seatbelts fastened when seated.

女士们，先生们：

现在客舱乘务员向您介绍(救生衣)、氧气面罩、安全带的使用方法和应急出口的位置。

救生衣在您座椅下面的口袋里，使用时取出，经头部穿好。

将带子从后向前系在腰上并扣好扣环、系紧。

在离开客舱前，拉紧红色的绳子给救生衣充气。

充气不足时，用嘴向人工充气管里充气。

氧气面罩储藏在您的座椅上方，发生紧急情况时面罩会自动脱落。

氧气面罩脱落后，请用力向下拉面罩。

将面罩罩在口鼻处，把带子套在头上进行正常呼吸。

在您座椅上各有两条可以对扣起来的安全带，将带子插进带扣，然后拉紧。

当您就座时，请系好安全带。

Part Ⅲ Words and Expressions

1. demonstrate [ˈdɛmənˌstreɪt] *vt.* 证明，演示，说明

2. oxygen [ˈɑːksɪdʒən] *n.* [化]氧，氧气

3. waist [weɪst] *n.* 腰，腰部

4. inflate [ɪnˈfleɪt] *vt. & vi.* 使充气

5. automatically [ˌɔːtəˈmætɪklːɪ] *adv.* 自动地

6. decompression [ˌdikəmˈpreʃən] *n.* 减压，解压；失压

7. activate [ˈæktəˌvet] *vt.* 使活动，起动，触发

8. elastic [ɪˈlæstɪk] *adj.* 有弹力的；可伸缩的

Part Ⅳ Reading Skills

保护嗓子的方法

保护嗓子的方法有以下几种：

1. 坚持锻炼身体，游泳和长跑是最有效的办法；

2. 科学练声，声音要由小到大，由近到远，从弱到强，从高到低；

3. 女性在生理周期或者因其他原因导致的身体不适时禁止练声；

4. 坚持以淡盐水漱口，可以消除炎症并保护嗓子；

5. 尽量少吃辛辣刺激性的食物，烟酒更要禁止。

Part V Practical Practices

1. Match the expressions in Column A with their Chinese equivalents in Column B.

Column A		Column B	
（1）	demonstrate	A	使充气
（2）	inflate	B	氧气
（3）	oxygen	C	演示
（4）	elastic	D	有弹力的
（5）	automatically	E	自动地

2. Translate the following sentences into English.

（1）氧气面罩放置在您座椅上方。

（2）当您就座时，请系好安全带。

（3）每位旅客座椅上都有一条可以对扣起来的安全带。

（4）请您全程系好安全带。

（5）救生衣仅供水上迫降时使用。

（6）请不要在客舱内为救生衣充气。

3. Translate the following sentences into Chinese.

(1) Your life vest is located under your seat.

(2) Oxygen mask will drop automatically in case of decompression.

(3) For ditching at night, a sea-light will be illuminated automatically.

(4) For further information, please refer to the safety instruction in the seat pocket in front of you.

4. Oral English practice

(1) Ladies and gentlemen,

We will now take a moment to explain how to use the onboard emergency equipment and locate the exits.

Your life vest is under/above your seat. It can only be used in case of ditching. Please do not remove it unless instructed by your flight attendant.

To put your vest on, simply slip it over your head, then fasten the buckles and pull the straps tightly around your waist.

Upon exiting the aircraft, pull the tabs down firmly to inflate your vest. Please do not inflate your vest while inside the cabin. For further inflation, simply blow into the mouth pieces on either side of your vest.

For ditching at night, a sea-light will be illuminated automatically.

Thank you.

(2) Ladies and gentlemen,

Now the flight attendants will tell you the location of your nearest exit. Please ensure two exits at least. Follow the instructions of the flight attendants and do not take anything while evacuating. If the exit cannot be used, move to another one immediately.

(3) Ladies and gentlemen,

May I have your attention please for the video of safety demonstration? If you have any questions, please contact our flight attendants.

Thank you.

Task 9　Security Inspection

Learning Objective

Knowledge Objectives

1. To know how to make an announcement about security inspection.

2. To learn some useful expressions about security inspection.

Skill Objectives

1. To master the keywords and expressions on security inspection.

2. To master a reading skill.

Quality Objectives

1. To develop the sense of professionalism and fighting spirit.

2. To be knowledgeable and professional.

Part Ⅰ　Lead-in

Question：

Passengers taking flight all expect to have a smooth journey. But emergency or special situations do sometimes happen whether they like it or not, so safety check is very important.

As a flight attendant, you are doing safety check in the cabin before takeoff.

The plane is going to take off, but a passenger wants to go to the lavatory. How would you do?

Part Ⅱ　Reading

Pre-flight Security Inspection

1. Ladies and gentlemen,

Now, please fasten your seat belts, stow your tray table, return your footrest to its initial position and put your seat back to the upright position. Please help us by opening the sunshades.

To ensure the safe operation of the navigation system, please make sure your cell phones and other electronic devices, including those with flying mode, are switched off. This is a non-smoking flight, please do not smoke on board.

We hope you enjoy the flight. Thank you!

起飞前安全检查

女士们，先生们：

现在，请您将安全带系好，收起座椅靠背、小桌板及脚踏板，将遮光板保持在打开的状态。

为了避免干扰通信导航系统的正常工作，请确保您的手机及具有"飞行模式"功能的所有电子设备已经处于关闭状态。本次航班全程禁烟，请勿在航班上吸烟！

祝您旅途愉快。谢谢！

Before landing Security Inspection

2. Ladies and gentlemen,

We are beginning our final descent. Please fasten your seatbelts, return your seat back to the upright position and stow your tray table, and return your footrest to its initial position. Please help us by opening the sunshades. All laptop computers and electronic devices should be turned off at this time. For your safety, we kindly remind you that during landing and taxiing, please keep your seatbelts fastened and do not open the overhead compartment. We will be dimming the cabin lights for landing. Thank you!

落地前安全检查

女士们，先生们：

我们的飞机已经开始下降，乘务员将进行安全确认。请您将安全带系好，收起座椅靠背、小桌板及脚踏板，将遮光板保持在打开的状态。请您关闭手提电脑及其他电子设备。为了您的安全，在飞机着陆及滑行期间，请不要解开安全带或打开行李架。稍后，我们将调暗客舱灯光。谢谢！

Part Ⅲ Words and Expressions

1. footrest ['futrest] *n.* 搁脚物；脚蹬

2. initial [ɪ'nɪʃ(ə)l] *adj.* 最初的；开始的；

3. sunshade ['sʌnʃeɪd] *n.* 阳伞；凉篷；遮光板

4. navigation [nævɪ'geɪʃ(ə)n] *n.* 航行；航海；航空；

5. descent [dɪ'sent] *n.* 下降；下落；

6. remind [rɪˈmaɪnd] *v.* 使记起；使想起

7. compartment [kəmˈpɑːtmənt] *n.* 船舱；隔间；车厢；

Part Ⅳ　Reading Skill

气息练习

俗话说"练声先练气"。气息练习的目的是体会和掌握胸腹联合呼吸的基本动作要领，形成新的、符合朗诵发声要求的呼吸方式。想要达成这一目的，只能坚持不懈、持之以恒地练习。练习时，注意要发音准确，出字要有力，咬住字头，拉开字腹，收住字尾；声音连贯，自如控制气息。

Part Ⅴ　Practical Practices

1. Match the expressions in Column A with their Chinese equivalents in Column B.

Column A		Column B	
（1）	operation	A	笔记本电脑
（2）	initial	B	运转
（3）	dim	C	最初的
（4）	mode	D	模式
（5）	laptop	E	（使）变昏暗

2. Translate the following sentences into English.

（1）本次航班全程禁烟，请勿在航班上吸烟！

（2）为了您的安全，在飞机着陆及滑行期间，请不要解开安全带或打开行李架。

3. Translate the following sentences into Chinese.

（1）To ensure the safe operation of the navigation system, please make sure your cell phones, including those with flying mode, are switched off.

(2) All laptop computers and electronic devices should be turned off at this time.

4. Oral English practice

(1) Ladies and gentlemen,

Now the plane will be taking off and the flight attendants will do safety check. Please fasten your seatbelts, stow your tray table, return your footrest to its initial position and put your seat back to the upright position. Please help us by opening the sunshades. Your cooperation will be appreciated.

Thank you!

(2) Ladies and gentlemen,

Welcome aboard flight _____ from _____ to _____ . Would you please check your ticket and boarding pass again to make sure you're boarding the right flight?

As you enter the cabin, we kindly ask you that take your seat as soon as possible to give room for other passengers who may be standing in the aisle behind you.

Your seat number is indicated on the bottom edge of the overhead baggage compartment. Please place your carry-on baggage in the overhead compartment.

Small or fragile baggage should be placed under the seat in front of you.

Please do not leave any baggage either in the aisle or near an exit door.

Thank you for your cooperation!

Task 10　Restrictions on Electronic Devices

Knowledge Objectives

1. To know how to make an announcement about restrictions on electronic devices.

2. To learn some useful expressions about restrictions on electronic devices.

Skill Objectives

1. To master the keywords and expressions.

2. To master a reading skill.

Quality Objectives

1. To develop the awareness of standard and normativity.

2. To be knowledgeable and professional.

Part Ⅰ　Lead-in

Questions：

1. Can passengers use cell phones during the flight?

2. How to charge your device during a flight?

Part Ⅱ　Reading

Broadcast about Restrictions on Eletronic Devices

1. Ladies and gentlemen,

Welcome aboard _____ Airlines flight _____ . Now the cabin door has been closed. To avoid interference with navigation system, please switch off your mobile phones and all electronic devices. Please fasten the seatbelts, ensure that your tables and seatbacks are in an upright position and open the window shades. Smoking is not allowed during the whole flight. We wish you have a pleasant trip.

Thank you!

女士们，先生们：

欢迎您乘坐_____航空公司的_____航班。现在舱门已经关闭，为了避免干扰通信导航系统，请您将手机或电子产品全部关闭。请您系好安全带，收起小桌板，调直座椅靠背并打开遮光板。我们提醒各位旅客，本次航班全程禁烟，祝您旅途愉快！

谢谢！

2. Ladies and gentlemen,

Please note certain electronic devices must not be used on board at any time. These devices include cell phones, AM/FM radios, televisions and remote control equipment including toys. All other electronic devices including laptop computers and CD players must not be switched on until fifteen minutes after take-off, and must be switched off when the seatbelt signs come on for landing.

Your cooperation will be much appreciated.

女士们，先生们：

请注意，我们的航班上禁止使用电子设备，包括移动电话、收音机、便携式电视及包括玩具在内的遥控电子设备。起飞后十五分钟内，笔记本电脑、CD 播放器等所有电子设备必须关闭。落地时，当安全带指示灯亮起，所有电子设备也必须关闭。

感谢您的合作！

Part Ⅲ Words and Expressions

1. restriction [rɪ'strɪkʃ(ə)n] *n.* 限制；管制

2. electronic [ɪˌlek'trɒnɪk] *adj.* 电子的，电子学的

3. device [dɪ'vaɪs] *n.* 装置，设备

4. cabin door 舱门

5. avoid [ə'vɔɪd] *v.* 避免

6. interference [ˌɪntə'fɪərəns] *n.* 干扰

7. navigation system 导航系统

8. turn off （把…）关掉

9. mobile phone 移动电话

10. ensure [ɪn'ʃʊə(r)] *vt.* 确保

11. upright ['ʌpraɪt] *adj.* 垂直的

12. position [pə'zɪʃ(ə)n] *n.* 位置

13. whole [həul] *adj.* 全部的

14. pleasant ['plez(ə)nt] *adj.* 令人愉快的

15. trip [trɪp] *n.* 旅程

Part Ⅳ   Reading Skill

如何培养声音的魅力?

在播音时,男士使用明朗、低沉、愉快的语调最具有吸引力;而女士则以柔和、愉快、明朗的语调为适宜。说话时要注意速度的快慢,咬字要清晰,发音要准确,段落要分清,声音的大小要适中、适度。如果想在播音中给人以明朗、畅快的感觉,就应该注意语言要清晰,语音、频率要稍高一些,转折音要柔和。同时,注重声音的大小,语调的高低,一定能为你的声音增色不少。练习呼吸时要有一定的呼吸储量,要口鼻共同呼吸,气沉丹田,呼吸自如。播音是要抒发一种情怀、一种心情,以引起听众的共鸣,所以应在正确理解、深刻把握稿件的基础上,全身心投入感情。

Part Ⅴ   Practical Practices

1. Match the expressions in Column A with their Chinese equivalents in Column B.

Column A		Column B	
(1) restriction	A	导航
(2) interference	B	干扰
(3) upright	C	位置
(4) position	D	垂直的
(5) navigation	E	限制

2. Translate the following sentences into English.

(1)请注意,某些电子设备在航班上禁止使用。

(2)祝您旅途愉快。

3. Translate the following sentences into Chinese.

(1)To avoid interference with navigation system, please switch off your mobile phones and all electronic devices.

(2) Please fasten the seatbelts, ensure that your tables and seatbacks are in an upright position and open the window shades.

4. Oral English practice

Ladies and gentlemen,

Cabin doors have been closed. According to CAAC regulations, lithium power bank should be turned off. You may use your small portable electronic devices, such as mobile phones, after setting to airplane mode. Mobile phones without airplane mode, interphones and remote control equipment are prohibited during the entire flight. Headsets and oversized laptop or tablet PC are prohibited in critical flight phases, such as taxiing, takeoff, descent and landing. In order to ensure flight safety, cigarette and equivalent smoking are prohibited in this flight.

Thank you!

Task 11　Declaration Card

Learning Objective

Knowledge Objectives

1. To know how to make an announcement about dedaration card.

2. To learn some useful expressions about declaration card.

Skill Objectives

1. To master the keywords and expressions.

2. To master an announcement of declaration card.

Quality Objectives

1. To develop the awareness of professional standards and professional norms.

2. To be knowledgeable and professional.

Part Ⅰ　Lead-in

Questions：

1. What preparation should one make if he wants to visit Australia?

2. What is the function of green and red lanes?

3. Can you list some of the prohibited items?

Part Ⅱ　Reading

Entry Forms

1. Ladies and gentlemen,

In order to speed up your arrival formalities at ＿＿＿＿＿ Airport, all passengers, including minors (who are not local citizens), are advised to complete all entry forms for Customs, Immigration and Quarantine before landing. If you have any questions, please contact the flight attendant. Thank you!

申报单和入境卡

女士们，先生们：

现在我们为您提供申报单和入境卡（除当地公民外，所有旅客都要填写入境卡）。为了缩短您在＿＿＿＿＿机场的停留时间，请您在飞机着陆前填好。如您有任何问题，请与乘务员联系，谢谢！

CIQ Card Distribution

2. Ladies and gentlemen,

We will be distributing the Arrival Card (Immigration Card/Customs Declaration Form/Health Declaration Form). If you have any problems filling in the form, please feel free to contact us and we will be glad to help you.

After landing, please hand the completed forms to the officials of the Customs and Immigration Authority. Thank you!

发放 CIQ 单据

女士们，先生们：

现在我们将发放入境卡（移民卡/海关申报单/健康申报表），请您在飞机下降前完成填写。如果您在填写时有任何问题，请随时告诉我们，我们非常乐意协助您。落地后，办理入境和海关手续时，请将填好的表格交给海关和移民局工作人员。谢谢！

Declaration Form

3. Ladies and gentlemen,

May I have your attention please? In order to speed up arrival formalities in Los Angeles International Airport, you are advised to fill in the forms for Customs, Immigration and Quarantine before reaching your destination. All forms are supposed to be filled out in English. All members of one family please use one Declaration Form. If you have any problems please ask our flight attendants.

填写入境申报表

女士们，先生们：

请注意，为了加快办理到达洛杉矶国际机场的手续，我们建议您在到达目的地前填写海关、移民和检疫表格。所有的表格都要用英文填写。家庭所有成员请使用一张"申报表"。如果您有什么问题，请咨询空乘人员。

Part III   Words and Expressions

1. immigration ［ɪmɪˈɡreɪʃ(ə)n］　n. 移民

2. quarantine ［ˈkwɒrəntiːn］　n. 检疫

3. Arrival/Departure Record Form　出/入境登记表

4. Customs Declaration Form　海关申报表

5. Customs and Immigration Authority　海关和移民局

6. formality ［fɔːˈmæləti］　n. 正式手续，仪式

7. entry forms　入境表格

8. export ［ɪkˈspɔːtˈ］　v. 出口，出境

9. import ［ˈɪmpɔːt］　v. 进口，入境

10. fill in the form　填写表格

Part IV   Reading Skill

情景再现练习

做情景再现练习时，需在符合稿件需要的前提下，以稿件提供的材料为原型，使稿件中的人物、事件、情节、场面、景物、情绪等在播音员脑海里不断浮现，形成连续活动的画面，并不断引发相应的态度、感情。做好情景再现练习，需要做好以下4个步骤。

1. 理清头绪。我们头脑里连续的活动画面开头是什么？接下去是怎么变化的？以后又怎样发展？结果是怎样的？哪里是重点的特写镜头？

2. 设身处地。设身处地主要是为了获得现场感，产生"我就在"的感觉。

3. 触景生情。在毫无准备的情况下，受一个具体的"景"的刺激，马上引起我们具体的"情"，而又完全符合稿件的要求。

4. 现身说法。既然稿件中的情景始终"我就在"，那么"我"需在情景再现的过程中将其转述出来。

Part V   Practical Practices

1. Match the expressions in Column A with their Chinese equivalents in Column B.

Column A		Column B	
（1）	immigration	A	出口
（2）	quarantine	B	手续
（3）	formality	C	海关
（4）	export	D	移民
（5）	customs	E	检疫

2. Translate the following sentences into English.

（1）现在我们将发放入境卡（移民卡/海关申报单/健康申报表）。

（2）所有的表格都要用英文填写。

3. Translate the following sentences into Chinese.

（1）If you have any problems filling in the form, please feel free to contact us and we will be glad to help you.

（2）All members of one family please use one Declaration Form.

4. Oral English practice

Ladies and gentlemen,

We will be distributing the Arrival Card (Immigration Card/Customs Declaration Form/ Health Declaration Form). If you have any problems filling in the form, please feel free to contact us and we will be glad to help you.

After landing, please hand the completed forms to the officials of the Customs and Immigration Authority.

Thank you!

Task 12   Transfer Flight Information

Knowledge Objectives

1. To know how to make an announcement about transfer flight information.

2. To learn some useful expressions about transfer flight information.

Skill Objectives

1. To master the words and expressions about transfer flight information.

2. To master a reading skill.

Quality Objectives

1. To develop the sense of customer first and standardized service.

2. To be knowledgeable and professional.

Part Ⅰ   Lead-in

Questions:

1. Where should the transit passenger go through transfer formalities?

2. Which of the following items do belong to transfer procedures for international flight?

Part Ⅱ   Reading

1. Ladies and gentlemen,

We will be landing at Chengdu Shuangliu International Airport about twenty minutes. Please be seated and fasten your seatbelt. Seat backs and tables should be returned to the upright position. If you have a connecting flight, you'll have to go to the domestic terminal after you have declared customs. It's just beside the international terminal.

Thank you.

女士们，先生们：

我们将在 20 分钟后抵达成都双流国际机场，请您坐好并系好安全带，收起小桌板，调直座椅靠背，转机的乘客请先去海关办理申报手续然后到国内航站楼候机，国内航站楼在国际航站楼旁边。

谢谢。

2. Ladies and gentlemen,

Our plane has landed at Shanghai Pudong International Airport. The local time is four o'clock. For your safety, please stay in your seat. Please use caution when taking items out from the overhead compartment. Your checked baggage may be claimed in the baggage claim area. The transit passengers please go to the connection flight counter in the arrival hall to complete the transfer formalities. Thank you for choosing Air China, and we wish you have a nice trip.

女士们，先生们：

我们的飞机已经降落在上海浦东国际机场。当地时间是四点钟。为了您的安全，请您待在座位上。从头顶行李架取出物品时，请小心。您的托运行李可以在行李领取处领取。过境旅客请到贵宾厅的转机柜台办理转机手续。感谢您选择国航，祝您旅途愉快。

Part III Words and Expressions

1. belonging [bɪˈlɒŋɪŋ]   *n.* 行李；所有物

2. claim [kleɪm]   *v.* 声称；索取

3. connect [kəˈnekt]   *v.* 衔接

4. declare [dɪˈkleə(r)]   *v.* 申报；声称

5. delivery [dɪˈlɪvəri]   *n.* 递送

6. formality [fɔːˈmæləti]   *n.* 手续

7. procedure [prəˈsiːdʒə(r)]   *n.* 程序；步骤

8. schedule [ˈʃedʒuːl]   *n.* 手续计划，时间表

9. transfer [trænsˈfɜːr]   *v.* (旅行中)转移，换乘；转让，转移

10. transit [ˈtrænzɪt]   *v.* 通过；运输；运送；转变

11. valuable [ˈvæljuəb(ə)l]   *n.* 贵重物品

12. degree centigrade   摄氏度

13. domestic terminal   国内候机厅

14. international arrival hall   国际到港大厅

15. security check   安检

Part IV　Reading Skill

得体的语言

在客舱服务中，迎接、问候乘客，回答乘客提出的问题或向乘客进行说服工作时等，都需要沟通。这时得体的语言就显得尤为重要。客舱服务中，对乘客的称呼既体现了乘务员的服务态度，也反映了对乘客的关注程度。称呼不当，会引起乘客的不满，甚至产生反感，从而影响沟通效果，降低服务质量。服务时，一般称男士为"先生"，称未婚的年轻女性为"小姐"，已婚女性和无法确定该女性乘客是否已婚时称其为"女士"。

Part V　Practical Practices

1. Match the expressions in Column A with their Chinese equivalents in Column B.

Column A		Column B	
（1）	declare	A	申报
（2）	procedure	B	换乘
（3）	transfer	C	国内的
（4）	domestic	D	递送
（5）	delivery	E	程序

2. Translate the following sentences into English.

（1）请收起小桌板，调直座椅靠背。

（2）您的托运行李可以在行李领取处领取。

3. Translate the following sentences into Chinese.

（1）If you have a connecting flight, you'll have to go to the domestic terminal after you have declared Customs.

（2）The transit passengers please go to the connection flight counter in the arrival hall to complete the transfer formalities.

4. Oral English practice

(1) Ladies and gentlemen,

We regret to announce that mechanical trouble has made it necessary for us to transfer to another aircraft. Please disembark with all of your personal belongings and follow our ground staff. We apologize for the inconvenience caused.

Thank you for your kind understanding and cooperation!

(2) Ladies and gentlemen,

Our captain has advised that due to congestion at the airport/airport staff striking/unfavorable weather condition/strong headwind/air traffic control, we are unable to land at the moment. Our aircraft is expected to land in about 20 minutes. We shall keep you updated with any further information as we receive it.

Passengers planning to transfer at/in _____ Airport, please contact our ground staff after landing to make necessary arrangements for you. They will help you with your connecting flight. If you require any further assistance, we will be glad to help you.

We apologize for the inconvenience and thank you for your understanding.

Task 13　Level Flight

Knowledge Objectives

1. To know how to make an announcement about level flight

2. To learn some useful expressions about flight safety check.

Skill Objectives

1. To master the keywords and expressions.

2. To master a reading skill.

Quality Objectives

1. To develop the sense of responsibility.

2. To be knowledgeable and professional

Part Ⅰ　Lead-in

Question：

Straight and Level Flight is flight in which a constant altitude and heading are maintained. Do you know what is level flight?

Part Ⅱ　Reading

Trip Plan（For Economy Cabin only）

Notice：

1. Ladies and gentlemen，

Our aircraft has left and been steady. We will provide you with a beverage and （breakfast/lunch/dinner/refreshment/snack）service shortly.

Long Haul：We will be landing after ×××hours（breakfast/lunch/dinner/refreshment）is about to be offered after ×××hours.（And the duty free sales will begin after the meal.）

Please keep your seat belts fastened when seated in case of sudden turbulence. Once again，all mobile phones need to be powered off during entire flight.（While using your personal laptop，please make sure the Wi-Fi function has been switched off．) We will be by your side any time you need anything from us．We wish you have a pleasant trip.

平飞广播

女士们，先生们：

飞机已进入平飞状态。我们正在为您准备饮料和早餐/午餐/晚餐/便餐/点心，稍后您就可以享用了。

远程航线：大约在 _____ 小时后 _____ 到达（目的地）_____ 小时 _____ 分钟，我们为您提供（早餐/午餐/晚餐/便餐。）（餐后，我们还将销售免税商品。）

为了防止意外颠簸，就座时请系好安全带。再次提醒您，旅途中请不要打开包括带有"飞行模式"功能的手机，（在您使用个人电脑时，请记得关闭无线网络功能。）如您需要服务，请随时告诉我们。祝您旅途愉快。

注意：在可分舱广播的机型上仅对普通舱使用该广播。

另外，在提供无线网络的飞机上不播报："在您使用个人电脑时，请记得关闭无线网络功能。"

Trip Plan on Night

2. Ladies and gentlemen，

To ensure a good rest，we will dim the cabin lights．If you would like to read，you may use the reading light over your head．As a precaution against sudden turbulence，we advise you to keep your seat belt fastened while seated．Please press the call button for service.

Thank you.

夜间飞行广播

女士们，先生们：

为了使您再旅途中得到良好的休息，我们将调暗客舱灯光，需要阅读书刊的旅客，可以打开您头顶上方的阅读灯。为预防突发颠簸，请您在就座期间系好安全带。如您需要帮助，请按呼叫铃。谢谢。

Part Ⅲ　Words and Expressions

1. provide sth for sb　提供东西给某人

   provide sb with sth　提供某人东西

2. beverage[ˈbevərɪdʒ] n. 饮料

3. refreshment［rɪ'freʃmənt］　*n.* 点心；起提神作用的东西

4. snack［snæk］　*n.* 小吃，快餐；一份，部分　*vi.* 吃快餐，吃点心，零食.

5. in case of　万一；如果发生；假设

6. portable［'pɔːtəb(ə)l］　*adj.* 便携的，可饮用的

7. function［'fʌŋkʃ(ə)n］　*n.* 功能

8. ensure［ɪn'ʃʊə(r)］　*vt.* 确保，保证

9. dim［dɪm］　*v.* 使暗淡

10. precaution［prɪ'kɔːʃ(ə)n］　*n.* 预防，警惕

11. turbulence［'tɜːbjələns］　*n.* 湍流

Part Ⅳ　Reading Skill

口腔控制练习

口腔控制练习要求字正腔圆，应做到以下几点。

1. 发音时，颧肌提起，似要唱歌的感觉，又似笑的感觉。此时口腔前上部有展开感，鼻孔也随之有些张大，唇也明显呈微笑状。

2. 牙关打开，才能使舌头活动范围增大，这样才更能清晰表达地字音，也给声音增加了明亮、刚劲的音色。

3. 软腭挺起，即软腭部分向上用力，这个动作可以使口腔后部空间加大，并减少灌入鼻腔的气流，避免过多的鼻音色彩。挺软腭可以用"半打哈欠"或"举杯痛饮"的动作来体会。

4. 在吐字发音的过程中，下巴向内微收，处于放松的状态，不能刻意，更不能着力。

Part Ⅴ　Practical Practices

1. Match the expressions in Column A with their Chinese equivalents in Column B.

Column A		Column B	
（1）　snack		A	确保
（2）　ensure		B	颠簸
（3）　turbulence		C	小吃
（4）　precaution		D	预防
（5）　portable		E	便携的

2. Translate the following sentences into English.

(1) 为了防止意外颠簸，就座时请系好安全带。

(2) 我们正在为您准备早餐与小吃。

3. Translate the following sentences into Chinese.

(1) Once again, all mobile phones need to be powered off during entire flight.

(2) As a precaution against sudden turbulence, we advise you to keep your seat belt fastened while seated.

4. Oral English practice

Ladies and gentlemen,

This is your purser speaking. Welcome aboard _____ Airlines.

The plane you are taking is Airbus 320. Now we are going to _____, the whole flight takes about _____ hours _____ minutes. We will be landing at our destination at _____ (time). This is our Golden flight. According to the regulation of CAAC, to be safe, we will provide cabin service 20 minutes after takeoff. Today we have prepared lunch and several beverages.

We have prepared some nice items for you. Please enjoy your shopping time later. For your convenience of travel, you can get the application forms of _____ Club and comment card from our cabin crew.

We may encounter some turbulence, please fasten your seatbelt when you are seated. And make the seatbelt outside your blanket to avoid being bothered.

We wish you a pleasant journey!

Thank you!

Task 14　Ground Temperature

Learning Objective

Knowledge Objectives

1. To know how to make an announcement about ground temperature.

2. To learn some useful expressions about ground temperature.

Skill Objectives

1. To master the keywords and expressions about ground temperature.

2. To master how to raise the awareness of the sincerity and enthusiasm of reading skills.

Quality Objectives

1. To develop the awareness of the sincerity and enthusiasm.

2. To be knowledgeable and professional.

Part Ⅰ　Lead-in

Question：

What would happen to the passengers if they feel uncomfortable due to the temperature in the cabin?

Part Ⅱ　Reading

Reminder of Cabin Temperature Oudside

Ladies and gentlemen,

Our plane has landed at _____ airport. The local time is _____ . The temperature outside is _____ degrees Celsius (degrees Fahrenheit).

The plane is taxiing. For your safety, please stay in your seat for the time being. Please don't open your mobile phone for now. When the aircraft stops completely and the Fasten Seat Belt sign is turned off, please detach the seat belt, take all your carry-on items and disembark. Please use caution when retrieving items from the overhead compartment.

Your checked baggage may be claimed in the baggage claim area. The transit passengers please go to the connection flight counter in the waiting hall to complete the procedures. It is raining/snowing outside, please be careful while getting out of the plane.

客舱外温度提醒

女士们，先生们：

我们已抵达_____机场，当地时间为_____。机舱外温度为_____摄氏度（_____华氏度）。

飞行还将滑行一段时间，为了您的安全，请在座位上耐心等候，请不要打开手机。在飞机完全停稳、安全指示灯熄灭后，请解开安全带，带好您的随身物品下机。下机时情小心打开行李架，以免行李滑落，您的托运行李请到候机楼行李提取处领取，需要转机的旅客请到转机台办理手续。外面正在下雨/雪，下机时请注意地面路滑。

Part Ⅲ   Words and Expressions

1. degree Celsius   摄氏温度
2. degree Fahrenheit   华氏摄氏度
3. disembark ［dɪsɪm'bɑːk］ *vi.* 离机；登陆，下车；上岸
4. detach ［dɪ'tætʃ］ *v.* 解开，折下，使分离
5. entry formalities   入境手续
6. caution ［'kɔːʃ(ə)n］ *n.* 注意；小心
7. retrieve ［rɪ'triːv］ *v.* 取回
8. ground temperature   地面温度
9. surface temperature   地面温度
10. baggage claim area   行李认领区

Part Ⅳ   Reading Skill

浊化

浊化就是把清辅音发成与其相对应得浊辅音。一般情况下，在音节开头如果有两个在一起的清辅音，那么第二个清辅音就要浊化，即发成浊辅音，常见的有 sp，st，sk，str。

1. ［sp］—［sb］

sport，space，speak，spoon，spray

2. ［st］—［sd］

stair, stand, start, steam, stick

3. [sk]—[sg]

skirt, skate, sky, ski, school

4. [str]—[sdr]

stream, street, strike, strict, string

需要格外注意，以下这些辅音组合在音节结尾或单词结尾时并不需要浊化，如 first, risk, mist, pianist, fist, bask, crisp, scientist 等。

Part V Practical Practices

1. Match the expressions in Column A with their Chinese equivalents in Column B.

Column A		Column B	
(1)	detach	A	取回
(2)	retrieving	B	注意、小心
(3)	degree Celsius	C	摄氏温度
(4)	caution	D	地面温度
(5)	ground temperature	E	解开

2. Translate the following sentences into English.

(1)为了您的安全，请在座位上耐心等候。

(2)外面的温度是 20 摄氏度。

3. Translate the following sentences into Chinese.

(1)When the aircraft stops completely and the Fasten Seat Belt sign is turned off, please detach the seat belt, take all your carry-on items and disembark.

(2)The transit passengers please go to the connection flight counter in the waiting hall to complete the procedures.

4. Oral English practice

Ladies and gentlemen,

We are waiting for clearance from air traffic control. We apologize that the air-conditioning is not working properly while the plane is still on the ground. It will be improved after take-off.

Thank you for your understanding and cooperation!

Task 15　Shopping

Learning Objective

Knowledge Objectives

1. To know how to make an announcement about shopping.

2. To learn some useful expressions about shopping in the cabin.

Skill Objectives

1. To master the keywords and expressions about shopping.

2. To master a reading skill.

Quality Objectives

1. To develop the sense of service.

2. To be knowledgeable and professional.

Part Ⅰ　Lead-in

Questions：

1. How to buy duty-free items?

2. How to give passengers suggestions on duty-free shopping?

Part Ⅱ　Reading

1. Ladies and gentlemen，

In an effort to further meet your traveling needs，we are pleased to offer you a wide selection of duty-free items. All items are priced in U. S. dollars. Please check with your cabin attendant for prices in other currencies. Most major currencies and U. S. dollar travelers checks are accepted for your purchases. The major credit cards are also accepted. Detailed information can be found in the Duty-free Catalog in the seat pocket in front of you.

女士们，先生们：

为了进一步满足您的旅行需要，我们很高兴为您提供种类多样的免税产品。所有商品均以美元计价。请向您的乘务员查询其他货币的价格。可接受大多数主要货币和美元旅行支票等支付方式。主要种类的信用卡也可支付。详细资料可在座位口袋前的免税商品目录内找到。

2. Ladies and gentlemen,

Good morning!

Continental Airlines introduces another special service for you on this flight: a unique shopping experience while flying.

Within the pages of the newest Continental Collection, you will discover an unparalleled collection of over 60 items from the world's most sought after names: jewelry from Misaki, Carolee and Swarovski, watches from Anne Klein and Kenneth Cole, toys, liquor, fragrances and cosmetics, are all available to purchase duty-free while on board and to take with you.

Look for a copy of the Continental Collection Catalog in the seat pocket on board. Your flight attendant will be pleased to assist you with your selection.

All prices are in U. S. dollars. Most major currencies, travelers checks and credit cards are accepted. Enjoy your shopping and flight. Thank you!

女士们, 先生们:

早上好!

大陆航空公司为您介绍另一项特殊服务: 独特的飞行购物体验。

在大陆版最新商品的收藏页面中, 有全球购最受欢迎的60多件商品的名字, 如米莎绮、卡罗琳和施华洛世奇的珠宝, 安妮克·莱因和肯尼斯·科尔的手表, 玩具, 酒, 香水和化妆品, 这些都可以免税购买并随身携带。这些都可以在客舱的座位前排座椅下方口袋里的大陆收藏商品目录中找到。乘务员非常高兴帮您选择。

所有商品价格按美元结算, 现行货币, 旅行支票和信用卡都可支付。祝您购物愉快, 谢谢!

Part Ⅲ　Words and Expressions

1. duty ['djuːti]　*n.* 责任, 关税

   duty-free item　免税商品

   duty-free shopping　*n.* 免税购物

   duty-free catalog　免税商品目录

   duty-free allowance　免税限额

2. selection [sɪˈlekʃ(ə)n]　*n.* 选择

3. purchase [ˈpɜːtʃəs]　*n.* (正式)购买, 采购

4. cash [kæʃ]　*n.* 现金

5. credit card　信用卡

6. unparalleled [ʌnˈpærəleld]　*adj.* 无与伦比的, 独特的

7. brand [brænd]　*n.* 品牌

8. jewelry ['dʒuːəlri] *n.* 珠宝

9. liquor ['lɪkə(r)] *n.* 酒，含酒精的饮料

10. fragrance ['freɪgrəns] *n.* 香水

11. perfume ['pɜːfjuːm] *n.* 香水；香味

12. cosmetic [kɒz'metɪk] *n.* 化妆品

13. accessory [ək'sesəri] *n.* 配饰，配件

14. confectionery [kən'fekʃənəri] *n.* 糕点

15. cigarette [ˌsɪgə'ret] *n.* 香烟

16. whiskey ['wɪski] *n.* 威士忌

Part Ⅳ Reading Skill

动词过去式和过去分词的读法

1. 当一个动词的词尾是清辅音时，在变过去式和过去分词时加 ed，读作[t]，如 asked，laughed。

2. 当一个动词的词尾是浊辅音时，在变过去式和过去分词时加 ed，读作[d]，如 sobbed，slimmed。

3. 以 t 和 d 结尾的动词在变过去式和过去分词时加 ed，读作[id]，如 waited，folded。

4. 以元音结尾的动词在变过去式和过去分词时加 ed，读作[d]，如 prayed。

Part Ⅴ Practical Practices

1. Match the expressions in Column A with their Chinese equivalents in Column B.

Column A		Column B	
（1）	selection	A	品牌
（2）	brand	B	酒
（3）	liquor	C	香水
（4）	perfume	D	选择
（5）	cigarette	E	香烟

2. Translate the following sentences into English.

（1）请向乘务员查询其他货币的价格。

（2）乘务员将很乐意帮助您进行挑选。

3. Translate the following sentences into Chinese.

(1) Look for a copy of the Continental Collection catalog in the seat pocket on board.

(2) In an effort to further meet your traveling needs, we are pleased to offer you a wide selection of duty-free items.

4. Oral English practice

Ladies and gentlemen,

For passengers interested in purchasing Duty Free items, we have a wide selection for sale on this flight. All items are priced in U. S. dollars. Please check with the flight attendant for prices in other currencies. Detailed information can be found in the Duty Free Catalog in the seat pocket in front of you.

Thank you!

Task 16　Meals

Learning Objective

Knowledge Objectives

1. To know how to make an announcement about meals.

2. To learn some useful expressions about meals.

Skill Objectives

1. To master the keywords and expressions about meals.

2. To master a reading skill.

Quality Objectives

1. To develop the awareness of the sincerity and enthusiasm.

2. To be knowledgeable and professional.

Part Ⅰ　Lead-in

Question：

1. When will the passengers be served?

2. What is the difference between the meal service of First Class and Economy Class?

Part Ⅱ　Reading

Catering Service

1. Ladies and gentlemen,

In a few moments, the flight attendants will be serving meal/snacks and beverages. We hope you will enjoy them. For the convenience of the passenger seated behind you, please return your seat back to the upright position during our meal service. If you need any assistance, please feel comfortable to contact us. Thank you!

供餐广播

女士们，先生们：

我们将为您提供餐食/点心餐及各种饮料，希望您能喜欢。为方便后排的旅客，在用餐期间，请您调直座椅靠背。如需要帮助，我们乐意为您服务。谢谢！

Meal Service

2. Ladies and gentlemen,

We will soon be serving breakfast/lunch/dinner. We are offering you a choice of bread and noodles. We have also prepared the Muslim meal and the vegetarian meal. If you have special requirements, please tell the flight attendants. Thank you!

膳食服务

女士们，先生们：

我们马上为您提供早餐/午餐/晚餐，我们为您准备了面包和面条，还为您准备了清真餐食和素食餐。如果您有特殊要求，请告知乘务员。谢谢！

Meal Service Announcement on Long-haul Flights

3. Ladies and gentlemen,

The meal will be served soon. We have a selection of chicken with rice and beef with noodles today. Welcome to make your choice. Please put down the table in front of you while we are serving you the meal. For the convenience of the passenger behind you, please return your seatback to the upright position during the meal service. Thank you!

长期飞行服务广播

女士们，先生们！

稍后将为您提供餐食。我们有鸡肉米饭和牛肉面条，欢迎选择。在我们为您服务的时候，请放下小桌板。为了方便后排的旅客，在用餐期间，请您调直座椅靠背。谢谢！

Part Ⅲ　Words and Expressions

1. meal service　餐食服务
2. flavor [ˈfleɪrə(r)]　*n.* 口味
3. menu [ˈmenjuː]　*n.* 菜单
4. starter [ˈstɑːtə(r)]　*n.* 头盘，开胃小吃
5. appetizer [ˈæpɪtaɪzə(r)]　*n.* 开胃菜
6. main dish/main course　主菜
7. dessert [diˈzɜːt]　甜点

8. short-haul flight　短途航班

9. long-haul fight　长途航班

10. VGML　vegetarian meal（non-dairy & egg）　素餐

11. VLML　vegetarian meal（containing egg & dairy）　西式素餐

12. AVML　Asian vegetarian meal　亚洲素餐

13. IVGML　Indian vegetarian meal　印度素餐

14. RVML　raw vegetarian meal　生蔬菜餐

15. FPML　fruit platter meal　水果餐

16. BBML　baby meal under two years old　两周岁以下的儿童餐

17. BLML　bland meal（light easily digested meal）　软食、清淡、低纤维素餐

18. CHML　childmeal　儿童餐

19. DBML　diabetic meal　糖尿病餐

20. GFML　gluten free meal　无麸质，无谷类餐

21. HFML　high fiber meal　高纤维餐

22. LCML　low calorie meal　低热量餐

23. LFML　low fat meal　低胆固醇，低脂肪餐

24. LPML　low protein meal　低蛋白质餐

25. LSML　low sodium/ no salt meal　低钠/无盐餐

Part Ⅳ　Reading Skill

意群

相邻的两词在意义上必须密切相关，同属一个意群。连读所构成的音节一般都不重读，只需顺其自然地一带而过，不可读得太重，也不可连续。（连读符号用"～"表示）。

当短语或从句之间按意群进行停顿时，意群与意群之间即使有两个相邻的辅音与元音出现，也不可连读。

Is ~ it a ~ hat or a cat?（hat 与 or 之间不可以连读。）

There ~ is ~ a good book in my desk.（book 与 in 之间不可以连读。）

Can you speak ~ English or French?（English 与 or 之间不可以连读。）

Shall we meet at ~ eight or ten tomorrow morning?（meet 与 at，eight 与 or 之间不可以连读。）

She opened the door and walked ~ in.（door 与 and 之间不可以连读。）

不过这也不是绝对的，很多连读规则都是地方性的，按其中一种方法读就可以。

Part V　Practical Practices

1. Match the expressions in Column A with their Chinese equivalents in Column B.

Column A		Column B	
(1)	snack	A	小吃
(2)	flavor	B	菜单
(3)	menu	C	开胃菜
(4)	appetizer	D	口味
(5)	dessert	E	甜点

2. Translate the following sentences into English.

(1)我们将为您提供餐食及各种饮料。

(2)如需要帮助，我们乐意为您服务。

3. Translate the following sentences into Chinese.

(1)For the convenience of the passenger seated behind you, please return your seat back to the upright position during our meal service.

(2)We have a selection of chicken with rice and beef with noodles today.

4. Oral English practice

Attention please. _____ Flight _____ to _____ will be delayed because of weather conditions at _____ . A further announcement will be made not later than 10：30. In the meantime passengers are invited to take light refreshments with the compliments of the airlines at the buffet in this lounge.

Task 17　Beverages

Knowledge Objectives

1. To know how to make an announcement about beverages.

2. To learn some useful expressions about beverages.

Skill Objectives

1. To master keywords and expressions about beverages.

2. To master a reading skill.

Quality Objectives

1. To develop the sense of responsibility and the awareness of service.

2. To be knowledgeable and professional.

Part　I　Lead-in

Questions：

1. What are the general knowledge of meal and drink service in the cabin?

2. What can we offer to the passengers for the meal and drink service?

3. How can we establish the service dialogues in the cabin?

Part　II　Reading

Beverage Service Announcement

1. Ladies and gentlemen，

We will be serving you tea, coffee and other soft drinks. Welcome to make your choice. Please put down the table in front of you. For the convenience of the passenger behind you，please return your seat back to the upright position during our meal service. Thank you！

饮料服务说明

女士们，先生们：

我们将为您提供茶、咖啡和其他饮料。欢迎选择。请把小桌板打开。为了方便后面的旅客，在用餐期间，请您调直座椅靠背。谢谢！

No Beverage Service Announcement

2. Ladies and gentlemen,

We are sorry to inform you that we cannot serve you hot drinks on this flight because the water system is out of order. However, we will be able to serve cold drinks. We apologize for the inconvenience caused. Thank you for your understanding.

不提供饮料服务声明

女士们，先生们：

我们很遗憾地通知您，由于热水器故障，我们不能在这次航班上为您提供热饮。不过，我们可以提供冷饮。我们对造成的不便深表歉意。谢谢您的理解。

Sale of Beverages

3. Ladies and gentlemen,

We will begin our beverage service shortly, followed by lunch(dinner). Whiskey and Brandy are available for purchase in the main cabin. Thank you.

出售饮料

女士们，先生们：

稍候我们将为您提供饮料服务，然后是午餐(晚餐)。主客舱有威士忌和白兰地可供购买，谢谢。

Part Ⅲ Words and Expressions

1. Drink Service　饮料服务
2. apple juice　苹果汁
3. orange juice　橙汁
4. tomato juice　番茄汁
5. mineral water　矿泉水
6. carbonated water　气泡水
7. soda water　苏打水
8. tonic water　汤力水
9. milk〔mɪlk〕　n. 牛奶
10. soft drinks　不含酒精的饮料
11. Coca-Cola　可乐，Pepsi　百事可乐，Sprite　雪碧

12. green tea　绿茶

13. alcoholic beverages　酒精饮料

14. fermented liquors　发酵酒精饮料

15. beer[bɪə(r)]　*n.* 啤酒

16. wine[waɪn]　*n.* 葡萄酒

17. red wine　红葡萄酒

18. white wine　白葡萄酒

Part Ⅳ　Reading skill

掌握好节奏

掌握好节奏应做到以下几点。

一是要有快慢之分；

二是要快慢交替进行；

三是要根据材料内容的情感需要分清主导节奏和辅助节奏。

Part Ⅴ　Practical Practices

1. Match the expressions in Column A with their Chinese equivalents in Column B.

Column A		Column B	
(1)	mineral water	A	汤力水
(2)	tonic water	B	矿泉水
(3)	alcoholic beverages	C	龙舌兰酒
(4)	beer	D	啤酒
(5)	tequila	E	酒精饮料

2. Translate the following sentences into English.

(1)我们将为您提供茶、咖啡和其他饮料。

(2)不过，我们可以提供冷饮。

3. Translate the following sentences into Chinese.

(1)We are sorry to inform you that we cannot serve you hot drinks on this flight because the water system is out of order.

(2) We apologize for the inconvenience caused.

4. Oral English practice

Ladies and gentlemen,

This is your purser speaking, Welcome aboard _____ Airlines.

The plane you are taking is Airbus 320. Now we are going to Shanghai, the whole flight takes about 2 hours 15 minute. We will be landing at 14:35. This is our Golden Flight. According to regulation of CAAC, to be safe, we will provide cabin service 20 minutes after takeoff. Today we have prepared lunch and several-beverages.

We have prepared some nice items for you, please enjoy your shopping time later. For your convenience of travel, you can get the application forms of Fortune Wings Club and comment card from our cabin crew.

We may encounter some turbulence, please fasten your seat belt when you are seated and make the seat belt outside your blanket to avoid being bothered.

We wish you a pleasant journey!

Thank you!

Task 18　Recreation

Knowledge Objectives

1. To know how to make an announcement about recreation.

2. To learn some useful expressions about recreation.

Skill Objectives

1. To master the keywords and expressions about recreation.

2. To master a reading skill.

Quality Objectives

1. To develop the attitude of the sincerity and enthusiasm.

2. To be knowledgeable and professional.

Part Ⅰ　Lead-in

Questions：

1. What kinds of in-flight entertainment system do we have on board?

2. How to introduce the in-flight entertainment system to the passengers？

Part Ⅱ　Reading

1. Ladies and gentlemen,

For your convenience of travel, we have prepared in-flight entertainment equipment that contains movies, games, books and other entertainments for you. When you finish using it, please put it into the seat pocket in front of you. We wish you a pleasant journey. Thank you.

女士们，先生们：

为了便利您的旅途体验，我们在机上为您配备了娱乐设备，内置电影、音乐、游戏、书籍等多种娱乐项目，设备放置于您的座椅口袋中，使用完毕后，请您放回原处。祝您旅途愉快，谢谢。

2. Ladies and gentlemen,

Welcome on board. To make your flight more enjoyable, this aircraft is equipped with Wi-Fi service and mobile phone service. We will let you know when you can connect during the flight. Live TV sport plus news from CCTV, BBC and more are also available on our entertainment system. Switch on your Wi-Fi and connect it to the network. You can use your laptop once the seat belt sign is off. Thank you!

女士们，先生们：

欢迎乘坐本次航班。为了使您的飞行更加愉快，这架飞机配备了 Wi-Fi 服务和移动电话服务。在飞行期间，我们会告诉您什么时候可以接通。在我们的娱乐系统上可以看到来自中央电视台、英国广播公司等频道的现场直播的体育节目及新闻。您可以打开 Wi-Fi 并将其连接到机上网络。安全带标志熄灭后，您也可以使用笔记本电脑。谢谢！

Part Ⅲ Words and expressions

1. entertainment ［ˌentə'teɪnmənt］ *n.* 娱乐；款待；招待

2. opera ［'ɒprə］ *n.* 歌剧，歌剧院

3. cinema ［'sɪnəmə］ *n.* 电影院

4. movie theater 电影院

5. pleasant ［'plez(ə)nt］ *adj.* 愉快的

6. equipment ［ɪ'kwɪpmənt］ *n.* 设施，设备

7. connect ［kə'nekt］ *v.* 连接；联结

8. laptop ［'læptɒp］ *n.* 笔记本电脑；便携式电脑

Part Ⅳ Reading Skill

名词复数及动词第三人称单数的读法

1. 以［s］、［z］、［ʃ］、［ʒ］、［tʃ］、［dʒ］结尾的单词在变复数或第三人称单数时加 es，读作［iz］，例如：buses、mazes、washes、matches、bridges。

2. 除了以上音节结尾的外，所有以清辅音结尾的单词在变复数或第三人称单数时加 s，读作［s］，例如：books、hopes。

3. 其余所有以浊辅音或者元音结尾的单词在变复数或第三人称单数时加 s，读作［z］，例如：dogs、eyes。

4. 结尾是［t］音的单词在变复数或第三人称单数时，要将最后的［t］和［s］读作［ts］，例如：rests、lifts。

5. 结尾是［d］音的单词在变复数或第三人称单数时，要将最后的［d］和［z］读作

［dz］，例如：pretends, holds, friends。

Part V Practical Practices

1. Match the expressions in Column A with their Chinese equivalents in Column B.

Column A		Column B	
（1） entertainment	A	便携式电脑
（2） equipment	B	令人愉快的
（3） journey	C	设备
（4） laptop	D	旅程
（5） enjoyable	E	娱乐

2. Translate the following sentences into English.

（1）在飞行期间，我们会告诉你什么时候可以接通电话。

（2）当安全带指示灯关闭，您就可以使用笔记本电脑了。

3. Translate the following sentences into Chinese.

（1）For your convenience of travel, we have prepared in-flight entertainment equipment for you.

（2）Switch on your Wi-Fi and connect it to the network.

4. Oral English practice

（1）Ladies and gentlemen,

For your convenience of travel, we have prepared in-flight entertainment equipment for you. When you finish using it, please put it into the seat pocket in front of you. We wish you a pleasant journey.

(2) Ladies and gentlemen,

We are sorry that the video system is not available on this flight. We sincerely apologize for the inconvenience caused.

Thank you for your understanding!

Task 19　Landing on the Ground

Knowledge Objectives

1. To know how to make an announcement about landing on the ground.

2. To learn some useful expressions about landing on the ground.

Skill Objectives

1. To master the words and expressions about landing on the ground.

2. To master a reading skill.

Quality Objectives

1. To develop the sense of responsibility.

2. To be knowledgeable and professional.

Part Ⅰ　Lead-in

Question：

What can the attendants say when the flight is landing on the ground?

Part Ⅱ　Reading

Ladies and gentlemen,

We have just landed at Beijing Capital International Airport. It is 3:25 p. m. of November 20th by the local time. The temperature outside is 15 degrees Celsius (or 59 degrees Fahrenheit). Please remain seated until our aircraft stops completely. Please don't turn on your mobile phone. Please be cautious when retrieving items from the overhead bin until our aircraft stops completely. When you disembark, please take all your belongings. Your checked baggage may be claimed in the baggage claim area. (Passengers with connecting flights, please go to the transfer counter in the terminal.) For passengers bound for Macao, please prepare your passport and all your belongings to the terminal for exit formalities. Please pick up your luggage at the arrival hall. (Once again, we apologize for the delay of our flight. We thank you for your cooperation and understanding.) Thank you for choosing China Southern Airlines. It has been a pleasure looking after you and we hope to see you again. Thank you!

亲爱的旅客朋友们：

欢迎您来到北京首都国际机场！当地时间是 11 月 20 日下午 3 点 25 分，现在机舱外面温度为 15 摄氏度，59 华氏度。飞机还需要滑行一段时间，请保持安全带扣好，不要打开手提电话。等飞机完全停稳后，请您小心开启行李架，以免行李滑落发生意外。您的托运行李请去到达厅领取。前往澳门的旅客，请您准备好护照及全部手提物品到候机厅办理出境手续，（需从本站转乘飞机去其他地方的旅客，请到候机厅中转柜台办理。）（我们再次感谢您在航班延误时对我们工作表示理解与配合。）感谢您选择中国南方航空公司航班。我们期待再次与您相会，谢谢！

Part Ⅲ Words and Expressions

1. retrieve [rɪˈtriːv] *v.* 取回；索回

2. cautious [ˈkɔːʃəz] *adj.* 小心的；谨慎的

3. disembark [ˌdɪsɪmˈbaːk] *v.* 下（车、船、飞机等）

4. claim [kleɪm] *v.* 索取，索要（有权拥有的东西）；声称，断言

5. formality [fɔːˈmæləti] *n.* 正式手续

6. delay [dɪˈleɪ] *n.* 延迟（或耽搁、拖延）的时间

a delay of two hours／a two-hour delay 两小时的延误

7. transfer [trænsˈfɜː(r)] *v.* （使在旅途中）转乘，换乘，倒车

Part Ⅳ Reading Skill

弱读

通常情况下实词重读，虚词弱读。实词重读，如动词、名词、形容词、副词等；虚词弱读，如介词、代词、冠词、不定式符号等。

弱读的规则有以下两点。

1. 元音音节弱化成 [ə] 或 [i] 如下几个单词：for, as, at, of, the, to, as, than, and, or, his, a, an, but, been, for, her, we, be, shall, was, them 等。

例如，for [fɔː] 弱读为 [fə]；as[æz] 弱读为 [əz]。

2. 中元音[ʌ]被读为[ə]。

例如，some [sʌm] 弱读为[səm]；does[dʌz] 弱读为 [dəz]；but [bʌt] 弱读为 [bət]。

Part V   Practical Practices

1. Match the expressions in Column A with their Chinese equivalents in Column B.

Column A		Column B	
（1）	retrieve	A	谨慎的
（2）	cautious	B	索取、索要
（3）	disembark	C	下（船、飞机）等
（4）	formality	D	正式手续
（5）	claim	E	取回

2. Translate the following sentences into English.

（1）您的托运行李请去到达厅领取。

（2）下机时，请携带所有随身物品。

3. Translate the following sentences into Chinese.

（1）Please be cautious when retrieving items from the overhead bin.

（2）For passengers bound for Macao, please prepare your passport and all your belongings to the terminal for exit formalities.

4. Oral English practice

（1）Ladies and gentlemen,

Our airplane has arrived assigned position. Before leaving, please check to take all our carry-on baggage.

Thank you!

（2）Ladies and gentlemen,

We have arrived in Xi'an, the distance between Xi'an Xianyang International Airport and downtown is 47 kilometers. It is Beijing Time 15：30. The outside temperature is 28 degrees Centigrade.

We are taxiing now, for your safety, please turned off your mobile phone. In case of disturb communicate between cockpit and control tower, please do not open the overhead locker. When the airplane has come to a complete stop, we will brighten the cabin. Please open the overhead locker carefully, and then you can get ready for disembarkation. Thank you for flying with _____ Airlines and see you next time!

Task 20　Stopover

Learning Objective

Knowledge Objectives

1. To know how to make a in-flight announcement on stopover.

2. To learn some useful expressions about a in-flight announcement on stopover.

Skill Objectives

1. To master the keywords and expressions on stopover.

2. To master a reading skill.

Quality Objectives

1. To develop the sense of responsibility.

2. To be knowledgeable and professional.

Part Ⅰ　Lead-in

Discussion：

Stopover means landing at a place for a second time or loading goods on the way. When stopping, there are two arrangements for passengers on board.

Part Ⅱ　Reading

Domestic Stopover Flight Announcement

1. Ladies and gentlemen,

We have just landed at Jinan Yaoqiang International Airport. The temperature outside is 10 degrees Celsius, 50 degrees Fahrenheit.

Please remain seated until our aircraft stops completely and don't turn on your mobile phone. Please be cautious when retrieving items from the overhead bin. Passengers leaving the aircraft at this airport, please take all your belongings when you disembark. Your checked baggage may be claimed in the baggage claim area.

Those passengers continuing to Shenzhen, when you disembark, please take your ticket or boarding pass with you, and obtain a transit boarding card from the ground staff, then proceed to the waiting hall. We will be here for about 40 minutes. Your hand baggage may be left on board but take your valuables with you.

Thank you for flying with us. Have a pleasant day!

国内经停国内航班播音

女士们，先生们：

我们的飞机已经降落在本次航班的中途站济南遥墙机场，外面的温度是 10 摄氏度、50 华氏度。

飞机还需要滑行一段时间，请保持安全带扣好，不要打开移动电话。等飞机完全停稳后，请您小心开启行李架，以免行李滑落，发生意外。

到达济南的旅客，请带好您的全部手提物品下飞机，您的托运行李请在到达厅领取。

继续前往深圳的旅客，当您下机时，请带好您的机票或候机牌，向地面工作人员领取过站登机牌，到候机厅休息等候。我们的飞机将在这里停留 40 分钟左右，您的手提物品可以放在飞机上，但请您随身携带好贵重物品。

感谢您与我们共同度过这段美好的行程！

Home Stopover of International Flight

2. Ladies and gentlemen,

We have just landed at Dalian Zhoushuizi International Airport. The temperature outside is 10 degrees Celsius, 50 degrees Fahrenheit.

Please remain seated until our aircraft stops completely and don't turn on your mobile phone. Please be cautious when retrieving items from the overhead bin. Passengers leaving the aircraft at this airport, please take all your belongings when you disembark. Your checked baggage may be claimed in the baggage claim area. Passengers continuing to Hiroshima, please take your passport and all your belongings to complete the entry formalities in the terminal. Your checked baggage may be claimed in the baggage claim area.

Passengers continuing to Hiroshima, attention please! The aircraft will stay here for about one hour. When you disembark, please get your transit card from the ground staff, and complete your exit formalities and quarantine here. According to Customs regulations of the People's Republic of China, please take all carry-on items with you when you go through Customs. Any baggage left on board will be handed by the customs. Formalities for checked baggage will be complete at the customs counter.

Thank you for flying with us. Have a pleasant day!

国内经停国际航班播音

女士们，先生们：

我们的飞机已经降落在本次航班的中途站大连周水子国际机场，外面的温度是10摄氏度、50华氏度。

飞机还需要滑行一段时间，请保持安全带扣好，不要打开移动电话。等飞机完全停稳后，请您小心开启行李架，以免行李滑落，发生意外。

到达大连的旅客，请带好您的全部手提物品下飞机，您的托运行李请在到达厅领取。

继续前往广岛的旅客，请您准备好护照及全部手提物品在到达厅办理入境手续，您的托运行李请在到达厅领取。

继续前往广岛的旅客请注意：飞机在这里大约停留1小时左右。当您下机时，请向地面工作人员领取过站候机牌。请您在本站办理出境及检疫手续。根据中华人民共和国海关规定，请将您的全部手提物品带下飞机，接受海关检查。对遗留在飞机上的行李物品，将由海关人员处理。托运行李的手续将在海关柜台办理。

感谢您与我们共同度过这段美好的行程！

Part Ⅲ Words and Expressions 词汇打卡

1. boarding pass   登机牌
2. passport［ˈpɑːspɔːt］ *n*. 护照
3. transit card   过境证
4. exit formalities   出境手续
5. quarantine［ˈkwɒrəntiːn］ *n*.（为防传染的）隔离期；检疫

Part Ⅳ Reading Skill

名词复数读音规则

1. 在清辅音后读作［s］，例如：desk—desks map—maps。

2. 在元音和浊辅音后读作［z］，例如：dog—dogs tree—trees sea—seas。

3. 在 /t /，/d/后与前面的［t］，［d］连起来一起读［ts］，［dz］，如 cats, beds。

4. 以辅音字母 s, sh, ch, x 结尾的名词，在词尾加 -es，发［iz］，所以在［s］，［z］，［ʃ］，［ʒ］，［dʒ］，［tʃ］后发［iz］如 buses［bʌsiz］，blouses［ˈblauziz］，boxes［bɔksiz］，dishes［diʃiz］，bridges［bridʒiz］，watches［wɔtʃiz］。

Part V Practical Practices

1. Match the expressions in Column A with their Chinese equivalents in Column B.

Column A		Column B	
(1)	boarding pass	A	登机牌
(2)	passport	B	过境证
(3)	transit card	C	出境手续
(4)	exit formalities	D	检疫
(5)	quarantine	E	护照

2. Translate the following sentences into English.

(1) 对遗留在飞机上的行李物品，将由海关人员处理。

(2) 托运行李的手续将在海关柜台办理。

3. Translate the following sentences into Chinese.

(1) Your hand baggage may be left on board but take your valuables with you.

(2) Passengers leaving the aircraft at this airport, please take your passport and all your belongings to complete the entry formalities in the terminal.

4. Oral English practice

(1) Ladies and gentlemen,

We are sorry to inform you that we are heading direct to _____ Airport due to unfavorable weather conditions at _____ Airport (airport has been closed). We expect to land at _____ Airport at about _____ a. m. / p. m. We apologize for the inconvenience.

Thank you for your cooperation!

（2）Attention please!

Passengers continuing to other cities with _____ Airlines should take all your carry-on luggage and disembark. Please contact our ground staff for transfer procedures.

Task 21   Landing at the Destination Airport

Knowledge Objectives

1. To know how to make an announcement before landing at the destination airport.

2. To learn some useful expressions about flight safety check.

Skill Objectives

1. To master the words and expressions.

2. To master a reading skill.

Quality Objectives

1. To develop the sense of responsibility.

2. To be knowledgeable and professional.

Part Ⅰ   Lead-in

Question:

We are going to learn in-flight announcement before landing at the destination airport.

When we heard the flight attendant broadcast before landing, we feel very relaxed and relieved. Do you still remember what the attendants remind us to do, when the flight is about to descend?

Part Ⅱ   Reading

Ladies and gentlemen,

We will be landing at Harbin Taiping International Airport about 30 minutes. It is sunny in Harbin, the temperature is minus 10 degrees Centigrade and 14 degrees Fahrenheit. Because of the extreme weather difference, may we suggest you dress accordingly. The captain will switch on the Fasten Seat-belt sign soon. Would you kindly return to your seats, stow your belongings in the overhead compartments or under the seats in front of you, place your tray tables, footrests and seat-backs upright, check your seat-belts are securely fastened. All electronic devices must be switched off at this time. The lavatories and entertainment system will be closed in 5 minutes, the cabin crew will be coming around to collect your blankets and headsets, and we would appreciate if you would have them ready. The plane is about to descend, and according to the requirements of the China civil aviation regulations, we will stop all the cabin services, and the flight attendant will carry out the cabin safety inspection at a later time. At the same time, we would also like to remind you that please do not rise to open the overhead bin to pick up your luggage until the plane stops completely. Cabin pressure changes during descending, and if you feel ear pain, you can relieve it by swallowing.

Thank you!

女士们，先生们：

我们的飞机将在 30 分钟后到达哈尔滨太平国际机场。目前哈尔滨天气晴朗，地面温度是零下 10 摄氏度。请您及时整理随身物品，由于两地温差较大，建议您增减衣物。安全带信号灯即将亮起，洗手间和娱乐系统大约在 5 分钟后关闭，请将您不需要使用的毛毯和耳机交还给客舱乘务员。飞机即将开始下降高度，根据中国民航法规的要求，我们将停止一切客舱服务工作，稍后乘务员将进行客舱安全检查，为了您的安全，请您系好安全带、收起小桌板、调直座椅靠背将脚踏板放到正常位置、打开遮光板，乘务员将统一调亮客舱舷窗，请保持飞机舷窗在明亮状态。请关闭所有电子设备，下降及着陆期间请您将随身携带的小包放在前排座椅下方或行李架内。同时我们还要提醒您，在飞机完全停稳之前，请不要起身或开启行李架提拿行李物品。下降期间，客舱压力会发生变化，如果您感觉耳痛，可以通过吞咽动作来缓解。

谢谢！

Part Ⅲ　Words and Expressions

1. minus['maɪnəs]　*adj.* 小于零的；负的

2. stow['stəʊ]　*vt.* 装载

3. compartment[kəm'pɑːtmənt]　*n.*（飞机、火车车厢分隔成的）隔间，或（家具或设备等的）分隔间，隔层

4. entertainment[entə'teinment]　娱乐片；文娱节目；表演会；娱乐活动
   radio, television and other forms of entertainment
   广播、电视和其他形式的娱乐活动
   live entertainment　现场表演节目

5. descend[dɪ'əend]　下来；下去；下降

6. remind[rɪ'maɪnd]　*n.* 提醒；使想起

7. relieve[rɪ'liːv]　*vt.* 解除，减轻，缓和（不快或痛苦）
   to relieve the symptoms of a cold 减轻感冒的症状

8. swallow[ˈswɒləu] *vt.* 吞下；咽下

Part Ⅳ Reading Skill

如何掌握掌控气息，做到"以情运气"？

播音主持应"以情运气"，在播音中强调以情运气、气随情动。就是说不仅要准确认识和理解作品的思想内容，还要使思想感情随之运动起来，只有真正的动起来了，才可能做到气随情动，才能动得自如。在播音中如果总是用冷眼旁观的态度对待稿件，即使嗓音条件再好、呼吸再通场、基本功再扎实，播出来的东西，也是平平淡淡、毫无味道。所以，调动思想感情至关重要，只有思想感情动起来了，有了强烈的播讲愿望，呼吸才能自如地变化，语言也会富有色彩。语调生动，轻重适宜。根据需要，分出轻重缓急，分清抑扬顿挫，才能更好地表达出文章的思想感情。

Part Ⅴ Practical Practices

1. Match the expressions in Column A with their Chinese equivalents in Column B.

	Column A		Column B
（1）	centigrade	A	摄氏度的
（2）	belongings	B	关掉
（3）	inspection	C	随身物品
（4）	remind	D	检查
（5）	switch off	E	提醒

2. Translate the following sentences into English.

（1）由于两地温差较大，建议您增减衣物。

（2）洗手间和娱乐系统大约在 5 分钟后关闭。

3. Translate the following sentences into Chinese.

（1）At the same time, we would also like to remind you that please do not rise to open the overhead bin to pick up your luggage until the plane stops completely.

（2）Cabin pressure changes during descending, and if you feel ear pain, you can relieve it by swallowing.

4. Oral English practice

（1）Ladies and gentlemen,

We have arrived in _____, the distance between _____ Airport and downtown is _____ kilometers. It is Beijing Time _____ . The outside temperature is _____ degrees Centigrade.

We are taxiing now, for your safety, please turned off your mobile phone. In case of disturbing the communicating between cockpit and control tower, please do not open the overhead locker. When the airplane has come to a complete stop, we will brighten the cabin. Please open the overhead locker carefully, and then you can get ready for disembarkation.

Thank you for flying with _____ Airlines and see you next time!

（2）Ladies and gentlemen,

Our airplane has arrived assigned position. Before leaving, please check to take all your carry-on baggage.

Thank you!

Task 22 Seeing off

Knowledge Objectives

1. To know how to make an announcement about seeing off。

2. To learn some useful expressions about seeing off.

Skill Objectives

1. To master the words and expressions.

2. To master a reading skill.

Quality Objectives

1. To develop the sense of responsibility.

2. To be knowledgeable and professional.

Part Ⅰ Lead-in

Discussion：

When a flight lands on the ground, a lot of cautions should be mentioned by flight attendants besides the cozy greetings during seeing off the passengers.

Part Ⅱ Reading

Ladies and gentlemen,

Welcome to Xi'an. We will be arriving at Terminal 5 at Xianyang International Airport.

Please remain seated and keep your mobile phones switched off. Please do not open the overhead locker until the aircraft has come to a complete stop. Checked-in baggage may be claimed at the baggage carousel. If you are making a connection, please take all of your carry-on items and disembark. The ground staff will provide connecting information for you. For those passengers who are continuing to other cities abroad or domestic, please contact our ground staff. We are pleased to welcome you to our comfortable premium transfer lounge in Departure Hall of Terminal 5 for free. Our staff there are available to offer you best service.

If you are continuing to Lanzhou, please remain seated until we have further information for you.

All that remains for me to say at this time is to thank you for choosing to fly with South Airlines Company. And we look forward to seeing you again！Thank you！

女士们，先生们：

欢迎来到西安。我们的飞机停靠在咸阳国际机场 5 号航站楼。

飞机还需要滑行一段时间，请您不要站立，并保持手机电源关闭。等飞机完全停稳后，我们将调亮全部客舱灯光，届时请您整理好全部行李物品下机，开启行李架时请小心。您托运的行李请到机场到达厅提取。需要转乘航班前往其他城市的旅客，请根据地勤人员的中转指引，办理换乘手续。T5 航站楼二楼出发厅，为您准备了高端舒适的中转休息室，免费提供中转候机服务。如有疑问，我们的地勤人员很乐意为您提供帮助。

继续前往兰州的旅客，请您在座位上休息，先不要下飞机，我们将尽快广播告诉您后续的具体安排。

在此，我代表全体机组成员，感谢您选乘南方航空公司班机。南方航空公司期待与您再次同行！谢谢！

Part Ⅲ　Words and Expressions

1. staff[staːf]　*n.* 全体职工（或雇员）

   teaching staff　全体教师

   staff members　职工

   staff development/training　员工培养/培训

2. carousel[ˌkærəˈsel]　*n.*（机场的）行李传送带；旋转木马

3. premium[ˈpriːmiəm]　*adj.* 优质的；高端的

4. available[əˈveɪləb(ə)l]　*adj.* 可获得的；可购得的；可找到的

   available resources/facilities　可利用的资源/设备

5. offer[ˈɒfə(r)]　*v.* 主动提出；自愿给予

6. terminal[ˈtɜːmin(ə)l]　*n.* 航空终点站，航站楼；（火车、公共汽车或船的）终点站

7. look forward to　（高兴地）盼望，期待

Part Ⅳ　Reading Skill

动词过去式加 ed 的读音规则

动词加 ed 的读音主要有以下三种形式。

1. 以清辅音结尾的读[t]，如 worked, asked, helped, watched, stopped。

2. 以浊辅音和元音结尾的读［d］，如 rained，enjoyed，studied，moved，called

3. 以 t 和 d 结尾的读［id］，如 created，planted，wanted，needed

Part V Practical Practices

1. Match the expressions in Column A with their Chinese equivalents in Column B.

Column A		Column B	
（1）	staff	A	职工
（2）	available	B	自愿给予
（3）	offer	C	期待
（4）	expect	D	高端的
（5）	premium	E	可获得的

2. Translate the following sentences into English.

（1）请您不要站立，并保持手机电源关闭。

（2）您托运的行李请到机场到达厅提取。

3. Translate the following sentences into Chinese.

（1）We are pleased to welcome you to our comfortable premium transfer lounge in Departure Hall of Terminal 5 for free.

（2）All that remains for me to say at this time is to thank you for choosing to fly with South Airlines Company.

4. Oral English practice

Ladies and gentlemen,

We have just landed at _____ Airport Terminal _____ . The ground temperature is _____ degrees Celsius or _____ degrees Fahrenheit. Please remain seated with your seatbelt fastened and luggage stowed. The use of mobile phones is prohibited until the seatbelt sign is switched off. Be careful when you open the overhead compartments.

(We apologize again for the delay due to _____ .)

Thank you for flying with _____ Airlines and see you next time!

Task 23　Air Condition Problem

Knowledge Objectives

1. To know how to make an announcement about air condition problem.

2. To learn some useful expressions about air condition problem.

Skill Objectives

1. To master an announcement about loss of plosion.

2. To master a reading skill.

Quality Objectives

1. To develop the sense of responsibility.

2. To be knowledgeable and professional.

Part Ⅰ　Lead-in

Question and discussion:

Have you ever hear of an anouncement on air condition problem?

Part Ⅱ　Reading

1. Ladies and gentlemen,

As the air conditioning system of this aircraft does not work well on the ground, you may feel a little hot at the moment. We are sorry for this inconvenience. After takeoff, the cabin temperature will get down. Your understanding will be much appreciated. Thank you!

女士们，先生们：

由于本架飞机的空调系统在地面停留期间制冷效果不太理想，造成目前机舱温度较高，对给您带来的不适，我们深表歉意。这种情况在飞机起飞后会很快缓解。感谢您的理解，谢谢！

2. Ladies and gentlemen,

We are now waiting for the flight departure. You may feel a little bit hot now due to the air conditioning system doesn't work well before takeoff. We regret for this inconvenience at the moment. You may feel better after take off. Thank you!

女士们，先生们：

我们现在正在等待起飞，由于本架飞机在地面停留期间空调制冷效果不够理想，造成目前客舱温度偏高，给您带来不适，我们深表歉意，这种情况在飞机起飞后会很快缓解。谢谢！

3. Ladies and gentlemen,

Our flight is waiting for take-off because the engine has not been started, the air-conditioner cooling/heating system may not be effective during this period. We apologize for any discomfort due to the high/cold temperature.

This situation will be improved after taking-off. Thank you!

女士们，先生们：

我们的航班正在等待起飞，因为发动机尚未启动，在此期间空调冷却/加热系统可能无效。对于由于高温/低温而可能造成的任何不适，我们深表歉意。

这种情况在起飞后会得到改善。

Part Ⅲ　Words and Expressions

1. air-conditioner cooling/heating system　空调制冷/制热系统
2. inconvenience[ˌɪnkən'viːniəns]　n. 不便，麻烦
3. at the moment　此刻，当时，立刻，马上
4. appreciate[ə'priːʃieɪt]　v. 欣赏，鉴赏；感谢，感激
5. effective[ɪ'fektɪv]　adj. 有效的；起作用的；给人印象深刻的

Part Ⅳ　Reading Skill

失去爆破

当一个爆破音跟另一个爆破音相遇时往往失去爆破，这主要是因为两个辅音之间的间隔太小，这种现象在语音学上称为"失去爆破"。

1. 爆破音+爆破音＝失去爆破。

两个爆破音相邻，第一个爆破音只形成阻碍，但失去爆破，少停顿一下，快速向第二个完全爆破的爆破音划去，另一个在词尾的爆破音则必须轻化。请注意以下例句中的粗体部分的单词读音。

Write the answer in your **notebook**.

Please write the answer on the **blackboard**.

I'd like to say **goodbye** to everyone.

My father kept working till **midnight**.

The girl in the **red coat** was on a **black bike**.

The **big bus** from the factory is full of people.

What time does he **get up** every morning?

2. 爆破音+破擦音=失去爆破。

如爆破音后面紧跟着的是破擦音 [tʃ]，[dʒ]，[tr]，[dr]，[ts]，[dz] 时，这种辅音组合在语音学里叫作破擦爆破，换言之，即发爆破音时受后面的破擦音的影响爆破部位有所改变，须由口腔爆破改为破擦爆破，这时也就构成一种失去爆破。

I had my **picture** taken yesterday.

Do you know how to draw a **picture**?

You shouldn't treat women like **objects**.

He stood up and **objected** in strong language.

3. 不完全爆破。

爆破音和爆破音或其他的辅音相邻，第一个爆破音只形成阻碍，但不发生爆破，称作不完全爆破。说话时，前一个单词的爆破音只保持发音部位，而音不发出来时，即向下一个单词起音的辅音过渡，不完全爆破得以实现。不完全爆破产生的元音大体上是由于省力原则造成的。

Part V Practical Practices

1. Match the expressions in Column A with their Chinese equivalents in Column B.

Column A		Column B	
(1)	temperature	A	温度
(2)	air conditioning system	B	不便
(3)	inconvenience	C	改善
(4)	engine	D	空调系统
(5)	improve	E	发动机

2. Translate the following sentences into English.

(1) 由于本架飞机起飞前空调系统不能正常工作，您可能会感觉到一些闷热。

(2) 对给您带来的不适，我们深表歉意。

3. Translate the following sentences into Chinese.

(1) Our flight is waiting for take-off because the engine has not been started, the air-conditioner cooling/heating system may not be effective during this period.

(2) We apologize for any discomfort it may cause due to the high temperature.

4. Oral English practice

(1) Ladies and gentlemen,

This is your chief purser speaking. We are awfully sorry for the uncomfortable feeling caused by the cooling system of our flight. We thank you for your kind understanding, patience and cooperation. Thank you!

(2) Ladies and gentlemen,

With the excellent work of our crew and maintenance staff, the air-condition system is working properly now. You will feel better soon. We thank you for your understanding and cooperation. Now please be seated and ready for a safe takeoff. Thank you!

(3) Ladies and gentlemen,

It is very slippery outside because of rain. Please watch your steps as you disembark. Thank you!

Task 24　Flight Delay Announcement

Knowledge Objectives

1. To know how to make a flight delay announcement

2. To learn some useful expressions about flight delay.

Skill Objectives

1. To be able to identify levels of core skills and perform at the workplace.

2. To master a reading skill.

Quality Objectives

1. To develop the sense of responsibility.

2. To be knowledgeable and professional.

Part Ⅰ　Lead-in

Questions：

1. Have you ever listened to the delay announcements at the airport?

2. Do you know how to announce flight delay?

Part Ⅱ　Reading

1. Ladies and gentlemen,

I'm sorry to inform you that we have to wait another 15 minutes for takeoff because the runway is occupied.

Thank you.

女士们，先生们：

非常抱歉地通知大家，由于跑道占用原因，我们再过15分钟才能起飞。

谢谢。

2. Ladies and gentlemen,

I'm sorry to have to inform you that operational requirements have made it necessary for us to transfer to another aircraft. Please disembark with all your personal effects and follow our ground staff to the new aircraft. We apologize for the inconvenience.

Thank you for your cooperation.

女士们，先生们：

非常抱歉地通知大家，由于机械故障，现在决定换成另一架飞机。请您带好您的随身物品下飞机，随同地面值班人员去搭乘另一架飞机。对于给各位带来的不便，我们深表歉意。

感谢大家的合作。

3. Ladies and gentlemen,

May I have your attention please? China Eastern Airlines Flight MU582 to Shanghai will be delayed because of weather conditions at Hong Kong International Airport. A further announcement will be made not later than 10：30. In the meantime passengers are invited to take light refreshments with the compliments of the airlines at the buffet in this lounge.

女士们，先生们：

请注意。由于香港国际机场的天气原因，飞往上海的东航 MU582 次航班将延误起飞，何时起飞请听 10：30 之前的广播，现在请旅客们到候机室餐饮部免费享用航空公司提供的点心。

4. Ladies and gentlemen,

Japan Airlines regrets to announce the delay of the departure of Flight JL785 to Beijing. Due to technical reasons, this flight is now expected to depart at 10：40 local time.

女士们，先生们：

日本航空公司和很抱歉地通知各位，前往北京的日航 JL785 次航班将延误起飞。由于技术上的原因，预计该航班于当地时间 10：40 起飞。

Part Ⅲ   Words and Expressions

1. delay[dɪˈleɪ]　*vt.* 延误　延迟；延期；推迟

2. runway[ˈrʌnweɪ]　*n.* (机场的)跑道

3. occupied[ˈɒkjupaɪd]　*adj.* 使用中；有人使用(或居住)；忙于；被占领的；
被侵占的

occupy[ˈɒkjupaɪ]　*vt.* 使用，占用(空间、面积、时间等)；使用(房屋、建筑)；居住；侵占；占领；占据

4. operational[ˌɒpəˈreɪʃn(ə)l]　*adj.* 操作的；运转的；运营的；业务的

5. requirement[rɪˈkwaɪəmənt]　*n.* 要求；需求；必要条件

6. cooperation[kəʊˌɒpəˈreɪʃ(ə)n]　*n.* 合作；协作

7. refreshment[riˈfreʃmənt]　*n.* 饮料，点心(~s)，茶点

8. compliment[ˈkɒmplɪmənt]　*n. /v.* 赞扬；称赞

9. buffet [ˈbʌfeɪ]　*n.* 自助餐；（火车）饮食柜台；（车站）快餐部

10. lounge[laʊndʒ]　*n.* （机场等的）等候室 候机厅；

　　the departure lounge　候机室

Part Ⅳ　Reading Skill

语句重音

语句重音（sentence stress）是指根据不同的交际需要而对句子的某个或者某些词加以强调。重音的特点是发音用力较多，音量较大，时间较长。重音可分为表意重音、逻辑重音及情感重音。

1. 表意重音：表意重音是指讲话人在没有受个人情感影响或没有特意将句中的某一信息加以强调的情况下，对句中所有实词一视同仁地加以强调。实词包括：名词、动词、形容词、副词、数词、指示代词、疑问代词等；虚词包括：介词、冠词、助动词、连词、人称代词等。如：

a. In general, we emphasize a word as we stress a syllable by giving it more force, longer duration, and higher pitch.

b. I believe the course I have followed with China is the one that's best for America, disagreeing where we have serious disagreements, pursuing our common interests where I thought it was in the interest of the United States. （Bill Clinton）

2. 逻辑重音：逻辑重音又叫对比重音，指讲话人有意将句中的某个成分（一般只有一个，但也有两个的情况）与上下文当中的另一个成分相对比而给予的特殊强调。此时，句中本来该重读的实词被读得快而弱，本来该弱读的虚词被减弱到几乎听不出来的程度。试比较下组 7 个句子（重读有下画线的词）：

a. I suggest you talk to her this evening.

b. I suggest you talk to her this evening.

c. I suggest you talk to her this evening.

d. I suggest you talk to her this evening.

e. I suggest you talk to her this evening.

f. I suggest you talk to her this evening.

g. I suggest you talk to her this evening.

3. 情感重音是指说话人在处于极为激动的情况下，对某个能表达其情感的词或词组给予超常规的强调。如：We Chinese people are unconquerable!

Part V Practical Practice

1. Match the expressions in Column A with their Chinese equivalents in Column B.

Column A		Column B	
(1)	delay	A	转移
(2)	transfer	B	候机厅
(3)	refreshments	C	合作
(4)	lounge	D	点心
(5)	cooperation	E	延误

2. Translate the following sentences into English.

(1) 何时起飞请听 10：30 之前的广播。

(2) 由于香港国际机场上的天气原因，飞往上海的东航 MU582 次航班将延误起飞。

3. Translate the following sentences into Chinese.

(1) I'm sorry to inform you that we have to wait another 15 minutes for takeoff because of the runway is occupied.

(2) Please disembark with all your personal effects and follow our ground staff to the new aircraft.

4. Oral English practice

(1) Ladies and gentlemen,

We sincerely apologize for the delay due to _____ (unfavorable weather conditions/

aircraft late arrival/ air traffic control/ airport congestion/ mechanical problems/ waiting for some passengers).

Together with my team, we will try our best to make the rest of your journey as pleasant and comfortable as possible.

We thank you for your patience and understanding.

(2) Ladies and gentlemen,

We are still waiting for the boarding bridge (uttle bus/ ramp). Please remain seated, and we will inform you to disembark as soon as the air bridge arrives. Thank you for your understanding.

Task 25　Air Traffic Control

Knowledge Objectives

1. To know how to make an announcement about air traffic control.

2. To learn some useful expressions about air traffic control .

Skill Objectives

1. To master the key words and expressions.

2. To master a reading skills.

Quality Objectives

1. To develop the sense of responsibility.

2. To be knowledgeable and professional.

Part Ⅰ　Lead-in

Question：

Flight delay happens very constantly. If it happens, what shall we do after flight delay announcement?

Part Ⅱ　Reading

Waiting on Board Due to Air Traffic Control

1. Ladies and gentlemen,

Due to air traffic control, we haven't been informed about the time of departure yet.

Please wait for a moment until we have further information for you. We will be serving food and beverages while we are waiting for departure. Thank you!

因航空管制导致的机上等候

女士们，先生们：

由于航路交通管制，目前我们暂时还无法确定起飞时间，请大家在座位上休息等候，如有进一步的消息，我们会尽快通知您。在此期间，我们将为您提供餐饮服务。谢谢您的理解与配合！

Waiting on Board Due to Mechanical Problem

2. Ladies and gentlemen,

The captain has informed us that due to a minor mechanical problem with this aircraft that our departure will be delayed. Our maintenance staff is working diligently to solve this problem. As your safety is our primary concern, please remain in your seat. Further information will be provided as soon as possible. Thank you for your understanding and patience!

因飞机故障导致的机上等候

女士们，先生们：

非常抱歉地通知您，由于飞机故障，飞机将推迟起飞，对此我们深表歉意。机组和维修人员会尽快排除故障，为了您的安全，请您在座位上休息等候，进一步的消息我们将随时广播通知您。谢谢您的谅解和支持！

Announcement about the Balance of the Aircraft

3. Ladies and gentlemen,

May I have your attention please? For the balance of the aircraft, please follow the instructions of our ground staff, sit after row16. Thank you for your cooperation!

飞机配载平衡广播

女士们，先生们：

请注意！为了飞机起飞时的配载平衡，确保飞行安全，请您在地面工作人员的安排下在16排后就座。谢谢您的配合！

Announcement about Aborted Departure

4. Ladies and gentlemen,

The captain has aborted the take-off for safety concern. For your safety, please remain in your seat. We will give you more information as soon as it becomes available.

中止起飞广播

女士们，先生们：

由于安全原因，机长终止了起飞，请您在座位上保持安全带扣好。如有进一步的消息，我们将及时通知您。

Announcement about waiting for the（Shuttle Bus/Boarding Bridge）

5. Ladies and gentlemen,

Please remain seated while waiting for the shuttle bus/boarding bridge at Airport.

Thank you for your cooperation.

等待摆渡车或者廊桥广播

女士们，先生们：

由于摆渡车/廊桥未到，请您在座位上等待，感谢您的配合。

Part Ⅲ　Words and Expressions

1. instruction［in'strʌkʃ(ə)n］　*n.* 指示；指令；吩咐

2. minor［'maɪnə(r)］　*adj.* 较小的，次要的，轻微的

3. mechanical［mə'kænɪkl］　*adj.* 机械(方面)的；机械般的，呆板的

4. maintenance［'meɪntənəns］　*n.* 维护；保养

5. diligently［'dɪlɪdʒəntlɪ］　*adv.* 勤奋地；勤勉地
   diligence［'dɪlɪdʒəns］　*n.* 勤奋，用功

6. row［rəu］　*n.*（剧院，体育场等的）一排座位；一排，一行

7. abort［ə'bɔːt］　*vt.*（由于问题或故障）（使）夭折，中止（尤指很可能失败的事情）

8. safety［'seɪftɪ］　*n.* 安全；平安

9. concern［kən'sɜːn］　*n.* 影响，涉及，牵涉（某人或者某事）

10. primary［'praɪmərɪ］　*adj.* 主要的；最重要的；基本的

Part Ⅳ　Reading Skill

重读音节

音节是一个最小由元音组成的声音单位，但有可选的开始和结束辅音。音节通常承载着其他语音特征，如重音、音调和音高。简单来说，一个单词的音标中有几个元音就有几个音节。首先，一般来说，单音节词几乎都按重读音节对待。单音节

词多数是重读音节，标记读音时不需要使用重读符号。例如：

bag［bæg］   book［buk］   club［klʌb］

bird［bɜːd］   snail［sneɪl］   fish［fɪʃ］

pitch［pɪtʃ］   fridge［frɪdʒ］   school［skuːl］

任何双音节或多音节单词的音标中，有重读音节和非重读音节，哪一个音节重读，该音节的左上方或该音节的元音上方标有这样一个重读符号"ˈ"。例如：

worker［ˈwɜːkə］   actor［ˈæktə］

until［ənˈtil］   repeat［riˈpiːt］

Part V   Practical Practices

1. Match the expressions in Column A with their Chinese equivalents in Column B.

Column A		Column B	
(1)	temperature	A	温度
(2)	air conditioning system	B	不便
(3)	inconvenience	C	改善
(4)	engine	D	空调系统
(5)	improve	E	发动机

2. Translate the following sentences into English.

(1)由于本架飞机起飞前空调系统不能正常工作，您可能会感觉到一些闷热。

(2)对给您带来的不适，我们深表歉意。

3. Translate the following sentences into Chinese.

(1)As the air conditioning system of this aircraft does not work well on the ground, you may feel a little hot at the moment.

(2)We apologize for any discomfort it may cause due to the high temperature.

4. Oral English practice

（1）Ladies and gentlemen,

This is your chief purser speaking. We are awfully sorry for the uncomfortable feeling caused by the cooling system of our flight. We thank you for your kind understanding, patience and cooperation.

（2）Ladies and gentlemen,

With the excellent work of our crew and maintenance people, the air-condition system is working properly now. You will feel better soon. We thank you for your understanding and cooperation. Now please be seated and ready for a safe takeoff.

Thank you!

（3）Ladies and gentlemen,

It is very slippery outside because of rain. Please watch your steps as you disembark.

Thank you!

Task 26   Fasten the Seat Belt

Learning Objective

Knowledge Objectives

1. To know how to make an announcement about how to fasten the seatbelt.

2. To learn some useful expressions about fastening the seatbelt.

Skill Objectives

1. To master an announcement about seatbelt.

2. To master a reading skill.

Quality Objectives

1. To develop the sense of responsibility.

2. To be knowledgeable and professional.

Part I   Lead-in

Questions and discussion：

1. Do you know how the passengers have to fasten their seatbelts?

2. Have you ever heard of the most dangerous "11 minutes" while in the flight?

Part II   Reading

1. Ladies and gentlemen,

Each chair has a seatbelt that must be fastened when you are seated. Please keep your seat belt securely fastened during the whole flight. If needed, you may release the seatbelt by pulling the flap forward. You can adjust it when necessary.

When the "FASTEN SEAT BELT" sign is illuminated, please fasten your seatbelt. To fasten your seatbelt, simply place the metal tip into the buckle and tighten the strap. To release, just lift up the top of the buckle.

女士们，先生们：

每位旅客座椅上都有一条可以对扣起来的安全带，请您坐下后将安全带扣好并确认。如需要解开，只需要将金属扣向外打开即可。您可以根据需要自行调节长度。

当"系好安全带"灯亮时，请系好安全带，请将安全带一端的金属尖插入另一端的锁扣并调整好。解开时，请将锁扣打开，拉出连接片。

2. Ladies and gentlemen,

Our plane is descending now. Please be seated and fasten your seatbelt. Seat backs and tables should be returned to the upright position. All personal computers and electronic devices should be turned off. And please make sure that your carry-on items are securely stowed. We will be dimming the cabin lights for landing. Thank you!

女士们，先生们：

飞机正在下降。请您回原位坐好，系好安全带，收起小桌板，将座椅靠背调整到正常位置。所有个人电脑及电子设备必须处于关闭状态。请确认您的随身物品已妥善安放。稍后，我们将调暗客舱灯光。

谢谢！

3. Ladies and gentlemen,

Our plane is descending now. We expect to land at 8 : 00 P. M. on Beijing International Airport. Please fasten your seatbelt. I would like to thank you for flying with Air China. I do hope you have enjoyed your flight.

女士们，先生们：

我们即将开始下降，预计下午 8 点降落在北京机场，请系好您的安全带。本人谨代表中国航空公司及全体组员谢谢您的搭乘并祝您旅途愉快！

Part III Words and Expressions

1. seatbelt['si:tbelt] *n.* (汽车、飞机的)座椅安全带

2. flat[flæt] *n.* (附于某物的)片状下垂物，封盖，口盖，袋盖

3. adjust[ə'dʒʌst] *v.* 调整，调节；适应，习惯

4. illuminate[ɪ'lu:mɪneɪt]*vt.* 照明；照亮；照射

5. buckle['bʌk(ə)l] *n.* (皮带等的)搭扣，搭钩

6. strap[stræp] *n.* 带子，皮带；金属带；拉手吊环

7. upright['ʌpraɪt] *adj.* 竖直的；直立的；垂直的

Part IV Reading Skill

学会有节奏的朗读

英语的节奏是指英语音节在语流中强读和弱读的规律性。它以"步"(foot)为基础，每句话都有若干"步"，就好像音乐中的"小节"(bar)一样，每段乐曲都含有若干小节。乐曲中每个小节都以强拍开始；英语中，一般说来每一步的第一个音节都是重读音节。有的步单独一个重读音节组成，有的步由一个重读音节加上若干非

读音节组成。在朗读中，有的步有时也能以非重读音节开始，就如乐曲中的小节以休止符开始一样。这个步的非重读音节前也有个休止符，称为 silent beat。现在，我们用"/"表示步与步之间的界线。例如：

a. one/two/three/four/five

b. the/first of/April/nineteen/seventy/one/

每个人说话的速度各不一样，同一个人在不同的环境条件、使用不同的情绪时说话的快慢也各不相同。然而，在采用某一种语速的过程中，每步所需要的时间大致上是相同的，就像音乐中每个小节所占的时间相同一样，这就形成了节奏。为了保持节奏，包含音节多的步的语速就必须比包含音节少的语速快一些。因此，学生朗读课文，就必须懂得英语的节奏，自觉地实践。

Part VI Practical Practice

1. Match the expressions in Column A with their Chinese equivalents in Column B.

Column A		Column B	
(1)	upright	A	垂直的
(2)	dim	B	照亮
(3)	illuminate	C	搭扣
(4)	buckle	D	调整
(5)	adjust	E	（使）变暗淡

2. Translate the following sentences into English.

(1) 请系好您的安全带。

(2) 每位旅客座椅上都有一条可以对扣起来的安全带。

3. Translate the following sentences into Chinese.

(1) If needed, you may release the seat belt by pulling the flap forward.

(2) You can adjust it when necessary.

4. Oral English practice

（1）Ladies and gentlemen,

We will show you the use of life vest, oxygen mask, seat belt and the location of the emergency exits. Please give us your full attention for the demonstration.

Your oxygen mask is stored in the compartment above your head, and it will drop automatically in case of emergency. When the mask drops, pull it towards you to cover your mouth and nose, and slip the elastic band over your head, and then breathe normally.

（2）Ladies and gentlemen,

We have landed at Beijing International Airport, please remain seated until the "FASTEN SEAT BELT" sign is turned off and the aircraft has come to a complete stop. Please don't forget to take along your personal belongings. When opening the overhead bins, please take care to ensure the contents do not fall out. Once again, we would like to thank you for flying with Air China and hope to serve you again.

Words and Expressions

I 设备(Equipment)

1. 航空器设备 aircraft equipment

风挡 windshield/windscreen

机腹 belly-landing

(飞机的)外壳 skin

前部 front (fore) part

后部 rear (aft) part

左舷(舵)port-engine

右舷(舵)starboard-engine

内侧发动机 inboard engine or inboards

外侧发动机 outboard engine or outboards

(飞机的)引擎机舱 nacelle

轮舱 wheel well

主轮 main landing wheel

前轮 nose wheel

(大)机翼(main)wing

机翼前缘 leading edge

机翼后缘 trailing edge

翼尖 wing tip

操纵面 control surface

副翼 aileron

缝翼 slot/slat

升降舵 elevator

飞机方向舵 rudder

漏胎 flat tyre

(轮胎的)破洞 puncture

尾锥;机身末端 tail cone

天线 antenna

客舱 passenger cabin

地板 floor

顶棚（板）ceiling

机上厨房 galley

厕所 toilet

前（后）货舱 forward（after）hold

航行灯 navigation light

左（右）着陆灯 left（right）landing lamp

闪光灯 flash light

警告灯 warning light

2. 航空器系统（aircraft system）

（1）动力系统（powerplant system）

辅助动力装置 APU（auxiliary power unit）

引擎短舱 nacelle（engine cowling）

螺旋桨 propeller

（旧时用于旋翼机上的）风力旋轮，空气旋轮 windmill

外来物损伤 FOD（foreign object damage）

发动机失效 engine failure

发动机熄火 engine flame out

震动，颤动，抖动 vibration

马力小 the engine is low on power

发动机失灵 engine shutdown

发动机喘振 engine surge

振动 vibration

促动器；制动器 actuator

风扇 fan

气缸 cylinder

排气温度（exhaust gas temperature）EGT

（2）燃油系统（fuel system）

燃油箱 fuel tanks

燃油泵 fuel pump

燃油油压过低警告灯 low fuel pressure warning lights

煤油 kerosene

航空煤油 aviation kerosene

增压泵 boost pump

放油 fuel dumping/jettison

消耗 consume

油量不足 short of fuel

不充足 insufficient

剩余 remain

燃油增压泵 fuel booster pump

燃油（滑油）压力低 fuel（oil）pressure low（drop）

（3）液压（滑油）系统 hydraulic（oil）system

滑油温度表 oil temperature indicator

千斤顶（actuating）jacks

密封圈 seals

阀，活门 valve

（4）电器系统（electrical system）

发电机 generator motor

无线电设备 radio equipment

（备份）保险丝（spare）fuse

电线 wire

插头 plug

电路 circuit

跳开关 circuit breaker

电池电压 battery voltage

调压器 voltage regulator

（5）空调系统（air-conditioning system）

减压，释压 decompression

减压，释压 depressurize

失密 pressure failure

冷却 cooling

加热 heating

氧气面罩 oxygen mask

流量 flow

驾驶舱加温 pilot cabin heat

（6）刹车系统（brake system）

刹车 brakes

刹车不可靠 the brakes are unreliable

刹车状况不好 braking action is poor

松刹车 brakes released

气刹车 pneumatic braking

手刹车 manual braking

（7）应急系统（emergency system）

灭火系统 extinguisher system

防冰系统 deicing system

超温（过热）overheat

发动机灭火瓶 engine fire bottles

翼除冰 wing deicing

3. 驾驶舱（cockpit）

（1）操纵系统（control system）

飞行操纵系统 flight control system

飞行管理计算机系统（FMCS）flight management computer system

人工操纵系统 manual controls

自动驾驶操纵系统 autopilot controls

仪表着陆系统 instrument landing system

中央操纵台 center console

操纵台 control stand

控制板 control panel

杆 levers/stick/column

操纵杆 control column

操纵手柄 handle

油门杆/推力杆 thrust levers

按钮或旋钮 knobs

开关 switch

曲柄（摇把）cranks

前轮转弯手操作盘 nose wheel steering hand wheel

机内通话 inter communication

耳机 head set

装载与配平系统 weight and balance system

（2）航空器仪表（aircraft instrument）

仪表 instrument/gauge/indicator

仪表板 instrument panel

顶部仪表板 overhead panel

主显示系统 primary display system

指示器(仪表)indicator

飞行指引仪 flight director

备份地评议 stand by gyro-horizon

发动机仪表 engine indicator

测高仪，高度计 altimeter

无线电高度表 radio altimeter

空速表 airspeed indicator

升降速度表 vertical speed indicator(rate of climb and descent indicator)

转速表 R. P. M(revolutions per minute)

刹车压力表 brake pressure gauge

(3)航空器动作(aircraft manoeuvre)

俯仰 pitch/tilt

横滚 roll

偏转 yaw

压坡度 bank the aircraft

抬(提)起 lift off/rotate

抬机头 pitch up the aircraft (to nose up)

推机头 pitch down the aircraft (to nose down)

大角度爬升 climb steeply

修正动作 corrective action

改平 level off

失速 stall

(使)快速旋转，(球)螺旋 spin

从失速中改出 recover from stall

急转弯 sharp turn

减慢(速度)slow down

跟踪 trail

II 气象(meteorology)

1. 云(cloud)

云底高 ceiling

少云 FEW 1~2/8，few

疏云 SCT 3~4/8，scattered

裂开云，多云 5 ~ 7/8，broken

满天云 8/8，overcast（continuous）

在云中 in cloud

断续云中 in and out of cloud

云在增加 cloud is building up

云在消散 cloud is clearing up/dissipating

积雨云 CB（cumulonimbus）

塔状积雨云 towering cumulonimbus

2. 能见度（visibility）

晴空 sky clear

薄雾 mist

轻雾 light fog

浓雾 dense fog

吹雾，平流雾 drifting fog

雾在消散 fog is clearing up

雾越来越浓 fog is getting worse

烟 smoke

烟雾 smog

沙暴 sandstorm

3. 风（wind）

地面风 surface wind

无风（静风）wind calm

微风 light wind

中速风 moderate wind

强风 strong wind

顺风 tailwind

顶风 headwind

侧风 crosswind

阵风 gust

阵风达 8m/s gusts up to 8 m/s

风向风速仪 wind-gauge

稳定风 steady wind

风向不稳定 variable wind

风越来越大 the wind is getting stronger

风切变 wind shear

风暴 storm

4. 颠簸（turbulence）

晴空颠簸 clear air turbulence

中度颠簸 moderate turbulence

严重颠簸 severe turbulence

平稳的 smooth

上升气流 up draught

下降气流 down draught

高空急流，喷射气流 jet stream

5. 降水（precipitation）

小雨 light rain

大雨 heavy rain

间歇性雨 intermittent rain

连续性降水 continuous rain

偶尔下阵雨 occasional showers

零零散散的阵雨 scattered showers

毛毛雨 drizzle

雪 snow

冻雨 freezing rain

雨夹雪，冻雨 sleet

飑（指突起的狂风或短时的风景）squall

飓风 hurricane

龙卷风 tornado

冰雹 hail

雷暴 thunderstorm

闪电光 flash of lightning

闪电 lightning

雹暴 hailstorm

雪暴 snowstorm

结冰 icing

6. 温度（temperature）

外界温度，大气温度 outside air temperature

温度在上升 the temperature is rising

温度在下降 the temperature is falling/dropping

温度稳定 the temperature is steady

7. 跑道道面状况 (runway surface condition)

在化的雪 melting snow

雪水(或半化的雪) slush

雪堆 snow drift

雪清除 snow clearance

跑道上有结冰 the runway is icy

冰块(跑道上结的一块块冰) ice patches

跑道湿 the runway is wet

跑道滑 the runway is slippery

积水 pools of water/ standing water

刹车效应差 braking action is poor

刹车效应好 braking action is good

刹车效应中 braking action is medium

Ⅲ　机场车辆 (airport vehicle)

地面车辆 ground vehicle/car

机坪车辆 ramp vehicle

引导车 following car

空调车 air condition car

运送乘客巴士 shuttle bus

大客车 coach

摆渡车 airport passenger bus/ferry

餐车 galley service truck

食品车(配餐车) catering truck

拖把 tow bar

机载客梯 air stairs/steps

地面电源车 ground power vehicle

气源车 pneumatic vehicle

救火车 fire engine(truck)

救护车 ambulance

急救车 first-aid

油车 tank car

供水车 water service truck

平台车 dolly

保安运货车 security van

牵引车 tractor

犁雪车 snow plough

吹雪车 runway snow blower

吊臂车 cherry-picker

起重机 crane

Ⅳ 地面相关设备与服务(relevant ground equipment and service)

服务设备 furnishing equipment

医疗服务 medical service

安全服务 safety services

航站楼,候机楼 terminal

客/停机坪 apron/ramp

廊桥(英)air bridge/loading bridge

登机口 passenger gate

海关 customs

传送带 conveyor

地勤 ground handling

飞机库 hangar

航空运货单 air way bill

登机(英)embark/board

轮挡 wheel chock

风挡刮水器(美)windshield wiper

风挡刮水器(英)windscreen wiper

下飞机,从飞机上卸下(英)disembark/unload

地面电源插座 external socket

地面电源 ground power

外部电源 external power

拔下地面(外部)电源 disconnect ground(external) power

接上地面(外部)电源 reset ground(external) power

气源 start air

供气 supply start air

拔下(接上)气源 disconnect(reset)start air unit

消防队 fire service/assistance

故障排除 trouble shooting/fixed

航空常用英语单词

V 关于非正常情况和紧急情况的词汇及词组

A

abort take-off/reject/abandon 中断起飞

active runway(runway in use)正在使用的跑道

adjust 调整

a flock of birds 一群鸟

aileron 副翼

airborne 升空

air conditioning smoke＝pack 空调冒烟

allocate 分配

anonymous call(letter)匿名电话(信)

anti-icing system inoperative 防冰系统不工作

attacked 攻

automatic direction finding system 自动指引系统

auxiliary 辅助

B

backtrack 调头

baggage loader 传送带

belly landing(gear up landing)机腹落地

bird strike 鸟击

birds ingestion 吸鸟

blast fence 气流挡板

bomb 炸弹

breaking action 刹车效应

braking action poor 刹车效应差

burn off 消耗

C

cabin fire 客舱失火

cabin temperature is rising 客舱温度升高

cargo fire/smoke 货舱失火/冒烟

caution wake turbulence 注意尾流

center of gravity to the rear 重心靠后

chemicals of industrial 化学品

cockpit window broken 驾驶舱窗户出现问题

commence 开始

conflict 冲突

converging 会聚

converging traffic 汇聚飞机

cough 咳

cracked 破裂

crane operating/hoist 吊车

D

debris/fragments(metal strips)碎片

decelerating 减速

dense smoke 浓烟

destination 目的地

detect 探测

detonate explosives 引爆炸药

deviate from the corridor 偏出走廊

discharge extinguisher(agent)喷射灭火瓶(灭火剂)

disease outbreak 疾病暴发

dispatched 派遣

distance 距离

ditching 水上迫降

drunk 醉酒

dumping(jettison)放油

E

electric smoke or fire 电器冒烟或火警

emergency braking 应急刹车

emergency descent 紧急下降

emergency evacuation 紧急撤离

emergency gear extension not available(failure)应急放轮不成功

emergency gear extension 应急放轮

emergency landing 紧急落地

engine failure 发动机失效

engine fire 发动机失火

epidemic/pandemic 流行病

F

fade area 盲区

faint 晕倒

fever 发烧

fighter 战斗机

fire engine/fire truck 救火车

flame out 熄火

flight strip printer 飞行进程单

fly around（go round，circumnavigate，detour，offset）绕航

forced landing 迫降

fuel leak out 漏油

fuel level is going down 燃油液面下降

fuel starvation 燃料不足

G

give way to 让路

glide path 下滑道

ground air 地面气源

ground power 地面电源

gun-launched area 火箭炮空地

H

heart attack/disease 心脏病

hijacker 劫持者

hurt badly＝injury 受伤

hydraulic pressure is dropping rapidly 液压压力快速跌落

hydraulic system leak 液压系统泄漏

hypertension lost consciousness 高血压失去知觉

I

illuminate 照明；用灯装饰

incursion 入侵

J

jammed stabilizer landing 稳定差陆装置受阻

L

level change on route 航路上高度改变

left or right at your convenience 左右随你

low pass 低空通场

M

make further checks 做进一步调查

make a short circuit 小航线

maneuver left or right 右左机动

mechanical failure 机械故障

military movement 军事活动

mistake = false = incorrect 错误

N

noise abatement procedure 减噪音程序

norestriction 无限制

nose gear steering inoperative 前轮转弯不工作

O

obese 肥胖

obstacle(obstruction)障碍物

opposite direction 相反方向

orbit 盘旋

organize 组织

overheat 超温

P

parallel runway（taxiway）平行跑道（滑行道）

pAX baggage identification 旅客行李识别

pAX evacuation 旅客撤离

pAX stairs/steps 旅客客梯

priority landing 优先落地

proceeding to 飞往，前往

prohibited area/forbidden area 禁区

Q

quarantine 隔离

quarreled 争吵

R

reason unknown 原因不明

reduce 减小

registered number. 注册号码

rest route unchanged 其余航路不变

returning(coming back)返场

revised app. clearance 修正的进近许可

S

same direction 同向

shiver 发抖

short of fuel 燃油短缺

sick 病

skid off (slide off)滑出

slight/moderate/severe/serious/turbulence 轻度(中度，严重)颠簸

smoke continue 烟雾继续

special flight 特殊飞行

stall 失速

stretcher 担架

stroke 中风

structure damage 结构损坏

swine flu 猪流感

T

tail strike 擦尾

taxi with caution 小心滑行

thunder-storm 雷雨

too close to the preceding aircraft 太接近前面飞机

transmitter 发射机

try to find the cause 试图查明原因

turbine blades 涡轮碎片

U

unaccompanied child 无人陪伴的儿童

unreported vehicle 未经报告的车辆

unsure position 不明位置

V

visual app 目视应用程序

volcanic ashes 火山灰

vortex 漩涡

W

warning light on 警告灯亮

wheel chair 轮椅

wheelchairs/handicapped 障碍人士

wheel well fire 轮舱失火

wind shear 风切变

work in progress ahead 前面正在施工

wrong direction 错误方向

VI   飞行中常用的单词

A

above cloud 在云上

adjacent to 靠近

advised 进一步

airborne 升空

aircraft status 状况

airway 航路

all stations 各电台

anti-icing system 防冰系统

approved 同意

apron 机坪

ask for 请求

as published-at the moment 暂时根据公布

at your own discretion 由你自己决定

available 有效的，可行的

B

back on course 回到航路

back track 180°调头

balance 平衡

ballast 压舱板

be held up 阻碍

behind 在后面

belongs to 属于

be stuck in 卡住

between 两者之间

bird strike 鸟击

birds ingestion 吸鸟

broken 断开

break break 断开

busy 忙

buildup 雷雨

C

cabin decompression 客舱释压

cabin altitude 客舱高度

cabin fire 客舱失火

cancel 取消

calm 镇静

cannot 不能

call sign 呼叫

change 改变

cargo conveyor belt 传送带

check 检查

moved to the rear part unbalanced 重心移动、后部不平衡

check again 再检查

clearance 许可

close 接近

closing from right 从右接近

commence 开始

comply with 遵守

congestion 拥挤

conflicting 冲突

cross 穿越

crew 机组

crowd 拥挤

circle to land 反向落地

collide 撞击(collisionn)

D

detailed taxi instruction 详细滑行指示

delays undetermined 延误未确定

displaced 内移

distress 遇险

ditching 水上迫降

don't sink 不要下沉

due to broken surface 由于道面破损

due to spacing 由于间隔

due to weight 由于重量

during push back 推机期间

E

effective 有效

encounter moderate turbulence 遇到中度颠簸

experiencing moderate turbulence 遇到中度颠簸

emergency 紧急

emergency descent 紧急下降

emergency service 应急设施

engine failure 发动机故障

established LOC 建立航道

expedite 加速

extinguish 扑灭

extend downwind 延长三边

expect higher level 预计高高度

expect 预计

estimate 预计

exit 出口，离开

F

facing west 面朝前面飞机

fast turn off 快速道

flame out 熄火

flight plan route 飞行计划航路

first convenient right 第一道口右转

follow-in front of 在前面

forced landing 迫降

freighter 货机

full call sign 全呼

further advised 进一步通知

G

gear is not down 轮未放下

glide slope(path) 下滑道

give way to 让路

ground staff 地面工作人员

go round gravity 绕航重力

H

holding area 等待区域

I

icy patches 冰片

identify 识别

immediately 立即

inoperative 不工作

instruction 指令

intercept 切入

intersection 交叉口；（道路）交汇点

initially 起始，最初

J

jammed 卡阻

L

leave frequency 脱波

leave this area 离开此区域

low pass 低空通场

lose time 消磨时间

M

maintenance 维护

make orbit right 右盘旋

maneuver 机动

miss turn off 错过快速道

monitor 监督/班长

moving 移动

N

navigation 导航

not below FL130 不低于 FL130

unsure of my position 位置不确定

north east 东北

north west 西北

nose gear 前轮

O

obstacle 障碍物

orbit 盘旋

overtake 赶上并超过(汽车或人);(发展或增速)超越,超过

P

parking on the apron 在停机坪

port engine 左发

position 位置

possible reason 可能的原因

present position 目前位置

prevent 预防

problem 问题

proceed to 前往

pull in to the left 停靠到左面

pull over to the left 停靠到左面

pull up 拉升

Q

queued up 排队

R

radial 径向线

runway visibility 跑道能见度

rapidly 迅速

reason unknown 原因不明

recommend 劝告,推荐

reduce 减小,降低

regulation 规章

replacement 替换件

request priority 请求优先

response 回答

resume 恢复

recleared 重新许可

request level change en route 请求航路高度改变

rescue 营救

revised 修正过的,经过修改的

responsibility 责任、职责

right track 右航迹

rising 上升

rudder 方向舵

S

short count 短数

sink rate 下沉率

skid off 滑出，偏出

slot time 离场时间

squawk 应答机

starboard engine 右发问题

strengthen security 加强安全

struck by lightning 遭闪电击

stuck 陷入

structure 结构

survivals 幸存者

suspected heart attack 疑惑有心脏病

T

take the second left 第二道口左转

thunderstorm 雷雨

threshold 跑道入口处

tow bar 拖把

track out 出航

transmitter 发射机

transmitting blind 盲发

turbulence 颠簸

U

unable to comply 不能执行

undercarriage 起落架

unknown traffic 不明飞机

urgency 紧急

V

vacate 脱离

vector 引导

verify 核实

visual check 目视检查

W

Why overshot? 为什么复飞？

work in progress 正在施工

Reference Answers

Task 1　Check-in and Departure

1. (1)H　(2)J　(3)G　(4)C　(5)A　(6)E　(7)D　(8)F　(9)C　(10)I

2. (1) Passengers on this flight please have your belongings ready and proceed to the counter No. 1.

(2) Passengers who have not gone through check-in formalities, please go to the check-in counter as soon as possible.

(3) Flight CA1234 will depart in 30 minutes.

(4) Flight CA1234 to Shanghai will be boarding in 20 minutes.

(5) Ladies and gentlemen, boarding for flight CA1234 to Shanghai will now begin.

(6) The gate number of CA1234 has been changed from 8 to 9.

3. (1)搭乘本次航班的乘客请从 12 号登机口登机。

(2)祝您旅途愉快!

(3)对给您带来的不便,我们深表歉意。

(4)这是对前往上海的旅客的最后一次通告。

(5)请大家注意一下好吗?

(6)请勿在大门外吸烟。

Task 2　Notice of Flight Cancellation

1. (1)J　(2)B　(3)I　(4)H　(5)A　(6)E　(7)C　(8)G　(9)D　(10)F

2. (1) Thank you for your understanding!

(2) I'm sorry to tell you that your flight has been canceled because of the poor weather condition at our airport;

(3) We sincerely apologize for this inconvenience caused.

3. (1)我们抱歉地通知您,您乘坐的前往上海 CA1234 次航班,由于天气原因,本次航班决定取消今日飞行。

(2)我们抱歉地通知您,您乘坐的前往贵阳的 CA1234 次航班,由于航班阻塞,本次航班决定取消今日飞行。

(3)本次航班重新调整时间为明日 13∶40。

Task 3　Baggage Arrangement

1. (1)C　(2)A　(3)B　(4)D　(5)E

2. (1) Your seat number is indicated on the bottom edge of the overhead baggage compartment.

(2) Small or fragile baggage should be placed under the seat in front of you.

(3) Welcome aboard.

3. (1) 请根据座位号入座。

(2) 请尽快就座，保持过道通畅，让其他旅客通过。

(3) 请确保您的行李安放在头顶的行李架上。

Task 4 Boarding

1. (1) B (2) C (3) E (4) D (5) A

2. (1) Welcome aboard Air China flight CA1234, from Tianjin to Guangzhou.

(2) We hope you enjoy the flight!

3. (1) 请您再次确认您的航班号和登机牌，以确保您搭乘航班无误。

(2) 乘务长携全体机组人员竭诚为您服务。

Task 5 Welcome Speech

1. (1) E (2) B (3) D (4) A (5) C

2. (1) We will be flying at the altitude of 10, 000 meters and the average speed is 800 kilometers per hour.

(2) Please make sure that your seat belt is securely fastened, and you refrain from smoking during the flight.

3. (1) 乘务长携全体机组人员竭诚为您服务。

(2) 为了保障飞机导航及通信系统的正常工作，在飞行起飞和下降过程中请不要使用手提式电脑。

Task 6 Flight Route Introduction

1. (1) A (2) E (3) C (4) B (5) D

2. (1) The distance between Tianjin and Guangzhou is 1080 kilometers.

(2) Breakfast and beverages have been prepared for you.

3. (1) 在飞行全程中可能会出现因气流变化而引起的突然颠簸，我们特别提醒您，请全程系好安全带。

(2) 如果您需要帮助，我们很乐意随时为您服务。

Task 7 Emergency Exit

1. (1) B (2) E (3) C (4) D (5) A

2. (1) Now the cabin door has been closed.

    (2) There are six emergency exits located at the forward, rear and middle of the cabin.

3. (1) 接下来我们将为您播放安全须知，敬请关注。

    (2) 为了您的安全，我们将为您介绍紧急出口的位置。

Task 8   Safety Demonstration

1. (1) C   (2) A   (3) B   (4) D   (5) E

2. (1) Your oxygen mask is located in a compartment above your seat.

    (2) Please keep your seat belts securely fastened when seated.

    (3) Each chair has a seat belt that must be fastened when you are seated.

    (4) Please keep your seat belt securely fastened during the whole flight.

    (5) Life vests can be only used for ditching.

    (6) Please do not inflate your vest while inside the cabin.

3. (1) 救生衣在您座椅下方。

    (2) 当客舱释压时，氧气面罩会自动掉落。

    (3) 夜晚在海上紧急迫降时，灯会自动点亮。

    (4) 如需更多信息，请参考座椅前方口袋里的安全说明书。

Task 9   Safety Inspection

1. (1) B   (2) C   (3) E   (4) D   (5) A

2. (1) This is a non-smoking flight, please do not smoke on board.

    (2) We kindly remind you that during landing and taxiing, please keep your seat belts fastened and do not open the overhead compartment.

3. (1) 为了避免干扰通信导航系统的正常工作，请确保您的手机及具有"飞行模式"功能的所有电子设备已经处于关闭状态。

    (2) 请关闭所有笔记本电脑和其他电子设备。

Task 10   Restrictions on Electronic Devices

1. (1) E   (2) B   (3) D   (4) C   (5) A

2. (1) Please note certain electronic devices must not be used on board at any time.

    (2) We wish you a pleasant trip.

3. (1) 为了避免干扰通信导航系统，请您将手机或其他电子设备全部关闭.

    (2) 请您系好安全带，收起小桌板，调直座椅靠背并打开遮光板。

Task 11   Declaration Card

1. (1) D   (2) E   (3) B   (4) A   (5) C

2. (1) We will be distributing the Arrival Card (Immigration Card or Customs Declaration Form/Health Declaration Form).

(2) All forms are supposed to be filled out in English.

3. (1) 如果您在填写时有任何问题，请随时告诉我们，我们非常乐意协助您。

(2) 家庭所有成员请使用一张"申报表"。

Task 12   Transfer Flight Information

1. (1) A   (2) E   (3) B   (4) C   (5) D

2. (1) Seat backs and tables should be returned to the upright position.

(2) Your checked baggage may be claimed in the baggage claim area.

3. (1) 转机的乘客请先去海关办理申报手续然后到国内航站楼候机。

(2) 过境旅客请到贵宾厅的转机柜台办理转机手续。

Task 13   Level Flight

1. (1) C   (2) A   (3) B   (4) D   (5) E

2. (1) Please keep your seat belts fastened when seated in case of sudden turbulence.

(2) We will provide you/with breakfast and snack service shortly.

3. (1) 再次提醒您，旅途中请不要打开手机。

(2) 为预防突发颠簸，请您在休息期间系好安全带。如需帮助，请按呼叫铃。

Task 14   Ground Temperature

1. (1) E   (2) A   (3) C   (4) B   (5) D

2. (1) Please stay in your seat for the time being.

(2) The temperature outside is 20 degrees Celsius.

3. (1) 当飞机彻底停稳后，待安全指示灯关闭后，请解开安全带，携带好所有随身物品准备下机。

(2) 需要转机的旅客请到转机台办理手续。

Task 15   Shopping

1. (1) D   (2) A   (3) B   (4) C   (5) E

2. (1) Please check with your cabin attendant for prices in other currencies.

(2) Your flight attendant will be pleased to assist you with your selection.

3. (1) 请在座椅后面寻找大陆航空公司为您提供的免税商品目录。

（2）为了进一步满足您的旅行，我们很高兴为您提供种类繁多的免税商品。

Task 16 Meals

1.（1）A　（2）D　（3）B　（4）C　（5）E

2.（1）The flight attendants will be serving meal/snacks and beverages.

　　（2）If you need any assistance, please feel comfortable to contact us.

3.（1）为了方便后排的旅客，请您在用餐时将座位调成竖直状态。

　　（2）我们有鸡肉米饭和牛肉面条，欢迎选择。

Task 17 Beverages

1.（1）B　（2）A　（3）E　（4）D　（5）C

2.（1）We will be serving you tea, coffee and other soft drinks.

　　（2）However, we will be able to serve cold drinks.

3.（1）我们很遗憾地通知您，由于热水器坏了，我们无法在这次航班上为您提供热饮。

　　（2）我们对造成的不便深表歉意。

Task 18 Recreation

1.（1）E　（2）C　（3）D　（4）A　（5）B

2.（1）We will let you know when you can connect during the flight.

　　（2）You can use your laptop once the seat belt sign is off.

3.（1）为了丰富您的旅途生活，我们在机上为您配备了娱乐设备。

　　（2）您可以打开 Wi-Fi 并将其连接到机上网络。

Task 19 Landing on the Ground

1.（1）E　（2）A　（3）C　（4）D　（5）B

2.（1）Please pick up your luggage at the arrival hall.

　　（2）Please take all your belongings when disembark.

3.（1）当拿取行李时，请您小心开启行李架，以免行李滑落。

　　（2）到达澳门的旅客，请您准备好护照及全部手提物品到候机厅办理出境手续。

Task 20 Stopover

1.（1）A　（2）E　（3）B　（4）C　（5）D

2.（1）Any baggage left on board will be handed by the customs

　　（2）Formalities for checked baggage will be complete at the customs counter.

3.（1）您的手提物品可以放在飞机上，但请您随身携带好贵重物品。

（2）在本机场下机的旅客，请您准备好护照及全部随身物品到到达厅办理入境手续。

Task 21　Landing at the Destination Airport

1.（1）A　（2）C　（3）D　（4）E　（5）B

2.（1）Because of the extreme weather difference, may we suggest you dress accordingly.

（2）The lavatories and entertainment system will be closed in 5 minutes.

3.（1）同时我们还要提醒您，在飞机完全停稳之前，请不要起身或开启行李架提拿行李物品。

（2）下降期间，客舱压力会发生变化，如果您感觉耳痛，可以通过吞咽动作来缓解。

Task 22　Seeing off

1.（1）A　（2）E　（3）B　（4）C　（5）D

2.（1）Please remain seated and keep your mobile phones switched off.

（2）Checked-in baggage maybe claimed at the baggage carousel.

3.（1）T5 航站楼二楼出发厅，为您准备了高端舒适的中转休息室，免费提供中转候机服务。

（2）感谢您选乘南方航空公司班机，不期而遇，相伴相惜。

Task 23　Air Condition Problem

1.（1）A　（2）D　（3）B　（4）E　（5）C

2.（1）As the air conditioning system of this aircraft does not work well on the ground, you may feel a little hot at the moment.

（2）We are sorry for this inconvenience.

3.（1）我们的航班正在等待起飞，因为发动机尚未启动，在此期间空调冷却/加热系统可能无效。

（2）对于由于高温/低温而可能造成的任何不适，我们深表歉意。

Task 24　Flight Delay Announcement

1.（1）E　（2）A　（3）D　（4）B　（5）C

2.（1）A further announcement will be made not later than 10：30.

（2）China Eastern Airlines Flight MU582 to Shanghai will be delayed because of weather conditions at Hong Kong International Airport.

3. (1) 非常抱歉地通知大家，由于跑道占用原因，我们再过 15 分钟才能起飞。

(2) 请您带好您的随身物品下飞机，随同地面值班人员去搭乘另一架飞机 。

Task 25　Air Traffic Control

1. (1) A　(2) D　(3) B　(4) E　(5) C

2. (1) You may feel a little bit hot now due to the air conditioning system doesn't work well before take off.

(2) We regret for this inconvenience at the moment.

3. (1) 由于本架飞机的空调系统在地面停留期间制冷效果不太理想，您可能会感到一些闷热。

(2) 目前机舱温度较高，对给您带来的不适，我们深表歉意。

Task 26　Fasten the Sea Belt

1. (1) A　(2) E　(3) B　(4) C　(5) D

2. (1) Please fasten your seat belt.

(2) Each chair has a seat belt that must be fastened when you are seated.

3. (1) 如需要解开（安全带），只需要将金属扣向外打开即可。

(2) 您可以根据需要自行调节长度。